Praise for Λ

"I recommend this powerful book by my dear friend, Rabbi Steve Leder. It is filled not with theory, but with time-tested wisdom that can only come from years of experience helping people. This is such a beautiful book! It is the voice of experience, from a wounded healer who is both realistic and hopeful. I love Steve Leder, I love his congregation, and I loved reading this book! But don't just read it, buy a copy for a friend."

— **Pastor Rick Warren**, #1 *New York Times* best-selling author of *The Purpose Driven Life*

"Steve Leder is an extraordinary man, with a heart full of grace and a soul generated by love. In this book, he teaches us how to not just survive suffering, but indeed, how to thrive from it."

— **Tavis Smiley**, PBS talk show host and #1 *New York Times* best-selling author of *The Covenant with Black America*

"Rabbi Leder has written an uplifting and hopeful work about the most difficult of subjects—how we can be transformed by the most difficult trials that face us during our lives. His stories and insights are deep and true. This is an important and very human book."

— **Les Moonves**, CEO of CBS Corporation

MORE
beautiful
THAN

BEFORE

MORE
beautiful
THAN
BEFORE

HOW SUFFERING
TRANSFORMS US

STEVE LEDER

HAY HOUSE, INC.
Carlsbad, California • New York City
London • Sydney • New Delhi

Published in the United States by: Hay House, Inc.: www.hayhouse.com®
• **Published in Australia by:** Hay House Australia Pty. Ltd.: www.hayhouse
.com.au • **Published in the United Kingdom by:** Hay House UK, Ltd.:
www.hayhouse.co.uk • **Published in India by:** Hay House Publishers
India: www.hayhouse.co.in

Cover design: Karla Baker • *Interior design:* Nick C. Welch

**Cataloging-in-Publication Data is on file
at the Library of Congress**

Tradepaper ISBN: 978-1-4019-6712-3
E-book ISBN: 978-1-4019-5313-3

10 9 8 7 6 5 4 3 2 1
1st edition, November 2017
2nd Hay House edition, August 2022

Printed in the United States of America

To Betsy, Aaron, and Hannah,
who are my life.

CONTENTS

GROWING

INTRODUCTION

There is a crack in everything.

— RALPH WALDO EMERSON

Every one of us sooner or later walks through hell. The hell of being hurt, the hell of hurting another. The hell of cancer, the hell of a reluctant, thunking shovelful of earth upon the casket of someone we deeply loved. The hell of divorce, of a kid in trouble, of Alzheimer's, of addiction, of stress, of aging; of knowing that this year, like any year, may be our last. We all walk through hell. The point is to not come out empty-handed. The point is to make your life worthy of your suffering.

To be human is to suffer, and there is profound power in the suffering we endure if we transform it into a more authentic, meaningful life. Pain is a great teacher, but the lessons do not come easily. I have had people whose spouses had affairs tell me that working through the infidelity brought them a renewed love and a renewed marriage, better and more real than before. I have also had people tell me just the opposite. "Do we love each other?" one woman asked me rhetorically. "Yes. Am I glad we stayed married? Sure. But it will never be the same, and it would have been much better if it had never happened." Whenever I'm tempted to dismiss pain as merely a step toward enlightenment, I think about a friend of mine who had cancer three times and said to me from his hospital bed before he died, "This much character I don't need!"

I do not intend to glorify suffering or suggest that the lessons we learn from pain are somehow worth the cost. But the truth is that most often for most people, real change is the result of real pain. This is a book about real pain in its many forms and the lessons it comes to teach.

As the senior rabbi of one of the world's largest synagogues, I have witnessed a lot of pain. It's my phone that rings when people's bodies or lives fall apart. The couch in my office is often drenched with tears, and there are days when an entire box of tissues is gone by late afternoon. I have tried to help thousands of people face their emotional and physical pain, and after 27 years of listening, comforting, showing up, and holding them, I thought I knew a great deal about suffering. The truth is, it wasn't until my own pain brought me to my knees that I could really understand the suffering of those who came to me wounded and afraid.

A few months after a frightening car accident from which I thought I had emerged physically unharmed, I was pulling into the garage at home when a herniated disc touched and burned a nerve in my spine. The pain was paralyzing. I could not step out of the car. The doctor said to call the paramedics. Instead of dialing 911, I used my upper body to drag my lower body inch by inch, writhing and screaming, across the oil-stained garage into the house, where I curled up and wept on the floor, fetal and begging for morphine. Through the seductive opioids, the surgery, more and more and more drugs, the exhaustion, the withdrawal, the depression, the fear, the bitterness of *why me? why now?* and the healing that followed, I learned a good deal more about pain, both physical and emotional, than a lifetime of witnessing others' pain had taught me.

At first, I did not take my pain seriously. I took painkillers, tried to hide the fact that I wasn't sleeping much, kept up my brutal pace at work, and grimaced whenever I stood up. After the surgery a woman who was a Temple trustee at the time called me and said, "You broke your back for the synagogue." Her words shot through me. She was wrong from a medical standpoint, but she was right spiritually. I was ground down by years of carrying the suffering of others and the begging, pleasing, encouraging, and cheerleading that fundraising required when others refused to believe. So what did I do just 10 days after spinal surgery? I allowed a doctor to shoot me up so that I could walk back out onto the stage and play my part.

It was the High Holy Days—the 10 holiest days of the entire year for Jews, and the Super Bowl for rabbis, especially in my case and especially that year. We had just finished a two-year renovation of our historic 1,800-seat sanctuary, a magnificent place of prayer created in 1929 by movie moguls Louis B. Mayer, the Warner brothers, Carl Laemmle, and other famous Hollywood luminaries. The congregation had spent the two years of the renovation in temporary worship space, but this year we were coming home to a stunning, inspiring place of prayer, its 140-foot golden, green, and tan dome speckled with colors diffused through enormous deep blue and crimson stained-glass windows and bathed in soft white light from above by 30-foot brass chandeliers dangling from the dome like earrings on a queen. The total project cost for the sanctuary and the rest of the campus would be 200 million dollars, 150 million of which I had raised so far through countless conversations, dinners, events, and meetings over a period of 10 years. I didn't really want to acknowledge it, but all that fund-raising, along with running such a large congregation with a staff of hundreds and 7,000 members, depleted me. I was spent and confused.

"You've got six hours," the head of the hospital's spinal team told me as he jabbed the needle in. "After that, you won't be able to stand." My wife was the only person to tell me I was wrong to be on the pulpit that night as the project I had worked so hard to make real was unveiled. She was the only one worried more about me than about the congregation's expectations of me. Even I was not worried about me. If the pain was a relentless teacher, the student was a relentless denier.

I made it through the evening, but afterward I continued to suffer terribly for months, trapped in my old ways—always there for everyone, always punching above my weight, the hardest, the longest, and the fastest—I knew no other way. And then there were the drugs. I spiraled, like millions of others, into the lethargy and depression of steroids and opioids—the pain was dulled, but the pain was still in charge.

"Weeds bring yellow birds."

The Canadian philosopher Marshall McLuhan often repeated the aphorism that "we don't know who discovered water, but it wasn't the fish." What he meant was that we are so close to our own lives, so immersed in our own reality, that we actually have the least perspective on it. Only when it's hooked, thrashing in a net, gills gasping, and flailing for breath, only then does a fish discover water. So too with us—only when pain suddenly jerks us out of our otherwise ordinary life do we discover something powerful and true about ourselves. I have seen this up close thousands of times in hospital rooms, cemeteries, criminal courts, homes, and my office as others sat upon what I call my couch of tears, weeping from deep within. Through sickness we discover the blessing of health, through loss we discover the true depths of love, through foolishness we know maturity and wisdom. Pain shocks us and propels us from where we thought we were—who we thought we were—to something far more real and true. When pain visited me, I knew intellectually that I was not making history. I was not the first middle-aged man to herniate a disc. But pain is not a matter of intellect—it is a matter of the spirit and a matter of the soul.

It took years for me to appreciate pain's victory. Now I am grateful for my defeat. It forced me to change my stubborn ways. It forced me to make peace with age, flesh, bone, decline, limitation, and the simple fact that we are all merely human. We can only do so much. Then we have to let go.

My pain forced me to stop many things. One of the first and most seemingly insignificant but symbolically powerful things I had to stop was my war with weeds. Yes . . . weeds. Ever since buying our current home 11 years earlier, I'd been obsessed with getting rid of the weeds on the large, very steep hill behind it. I wanted nothing but a blanket of perfect, dark-green ivy when I looked out my back windows. I tried sprays, potions, axes, shovels, a chainsaw, machetes, pitchforks, trimmers, loppers—you name it. For a decade, every few days I was up on that hill slipping, falling, cursing—bent over and at war with those weeds while my wife, Betsy, shook her head and futilely uttered a simple truth repeated by wives to their husbands for 5,000 years: "You know we could hire someone to do that."

About a month after my spinal surgery, I emerged from the narcotic and steroidal haze just enough to walk the few steps to the back patio and lie on a lounge chair. That's when I saw them: hundreds of tall, gangly weeds sprouting on the back hill—an insult to my infirmity. I could do nothing to combat this aggressive new crop of nature's unceasing will.

Then I noticed something else: a group of tiny yellow birds perched atop those once-hated weeds. For weeks their singing kept me company each afternoon as I tried to heal in the warm sun. The weeds I had beaten back for years now attracted those delicate, little yellow birds. Pain cracks us open. It breaks us. But in the breaking, there is a new kind of wholeness that emerges. From my brokenness, a new, beautiful mantra emerged: weeds bring yellow birds.

This book is a journey through pain in three stages: surviving, healing, and growing. It is an exploration of pain's fierce, liberating, sorrowful, comforting, ugly, beautiful truths; the deepest truths. The truth that when we must endure, we can endure; that we can be good even when we cannot be happy; and that the sun rises no matter how dark the night. The people you will meet along the way, the ancient parables and scientific insights I share, my journey and the journeys I have walked hand-in-hand with so many others, will, I hope, help move you from pain to wisdom. They say every preacher has one sermon, one truth that he delivers 100 different ways. Mine is to inspire in us all a life worthy of our suffering: a life gentler, wiser, and more beautiful than before.

Surviving

WHEN YOU MUST, YOU CAN

Courage is not having the strength to go on;
it is going on when you don't have the strength.

— **ATTRIBUTED TO THEODORE ROOSEVELT**

People can bear tremendous physical and emotional pain. The kind of pain the psalmist cries out from when he says:

> *I am feeble and utterly crushed;*
> *I groan in anguish of heart.*
> *I am weary with groaning;*
> *Every night I drench my bed,*
> *I melt my couch with tears.*
>
> — Psalm 6:6

The kind of pain felt by this wounded veteran, who has turned to poetry on his blog:

I have been Broken. I have been beaten.
The Drugs battle what I cannot. Morphine vs. Pain.
My Body is the Battlefield. My Sanity the Casualty.

— Ray Buettner

There is real wisdom in that old expression: *when you must, you can.* I have watched parents hold their little boy as he died. Watched them bury his wisp of a body, lifeless, pale, cold. And then, watched them go on. Not because they are extraordinary but because they are ordinary—like you and me.

Before their son died, Barry and Michelle knew that day would come. He was diagnosed with a rare condition called Menkes' syndrome, affecting about 1 in 100,000 to 250,000 newborns. This disease impedes an infant's ability to metabolize copper, a trace element necessary for life. There is no cure.

I showed up, which is really the only thing you can do when someone is suffering. There is nothing to say or do that matters more than just showing up. Every week I stopped by with coffee and muffins from the Starbucks down the street. We talked as they held their son who we knew would die within the next few months. We talked about how death might affect their older son, who was three at the time. I told them he would have an old soul for the rest of his life. And that has turned out to be true.

I once heard a lecture in Jerusalem by a rabbi who was the youngest child to survive Auschwitz. The most chilling thing he said was that there were no children in Auschwitz. No matter what your age (he was six), you became an adult as soon as you walked through the electrified barbed-wire fence. There were no children in Auschwitz.

You don't really become a grown-up until you suffer some sort of real and deep pain. This means that some children can become adults at six and some adults can remain children well into their sixties, until their parents die, or their own body fails in some critical way, or their child, the light of their eyes, succumbs to disease or death, or their life crumbles during a divorce or a business or moral failure.

I told Barry and Michelle that though it was not worth the price of their sadness, they would have another child they never would have had otherwise without this horrible tragedy. They did. A beautiful girl. Nothing would ever be worth their suffering, but neither was their suffering worthless. Barry, who became the president of my congregation 15 years after his son's death, stood up in a critical meeting during which the trustees were considering taking the greatest financial risk in the congregation's history and said, "The worst has already happened to me. I am no longer afraid of anything." It was courage born of great pain. Victory won through loss.

When I arrive at a cemetery to greet a family before a funeral service begins, I often take the mourners aside and say something that seems terribly obvious, but something they often tell me afterward helped them a great deal. I look them in the eyes and tell them, "There is nothing I can say to make this easier. Death is an awful part of life. This is one of those times when you just put one foot in front of the other until it's over. Just keep going. That is all you can do and that is all you must do. Put one foot in front of the other until today is over."

"I just can't" is sometimes the response.

"You can and you will, because you must," I tell them. Then I put my arm around them and walk with them into the chapel to say goodbye to someone they deeply love. Not once in 30 years have I witnessed someone fail to keep going, walking, moving forward, however painfully and slowly, through that terrible day . . . not once.

While I was writing this book far away from home in Italy, a young woman approached me at a lecture we were both attending on the famous art dealer Stefano Bardini and his alleged forgery of Renaissance masterpieces. A friend I was with had told her I was writing a book about pain and she immediately opened up to me, telling me she had just returned from visiting her mother in England who was recovering from a bilateral mastectomy. I find that when most people, even total strangers, hear about the topic of this book, they often want to tell me about something painful that has happened to them. It is the most remarkable thing. People want to pour it out. People need to pour it out.

I told this young woman, so worried about her mother so far away, that the title of this book's first chapter was "When You Must, You Can." "That is what you should tell your mother, your father, and yourself," I urged her. "I am not talking about superhuman feats we sometimes hear of, like someone cutting off his own arm with a pocket knife in order to rescue himself from being pinned between two boulders. I am merely telling you that your mother and your dad will amaze you with how strong they can be because of how strong they must be."

I asked her how long her parents had been married. When she said 30 years, I reminded her that they had already been through a great deal by now. "Ask them what the most difficult thing is that they have ever faced and I will bet you that your mother's recent surgery is not it," I suggested to her. "Remind your parents and remind yourself that they had the internal strength, love, and courage to survive their previous pain, and therefore they have what it will take to survive this. This is called faith, and faith in oneself and loved ones is so important.

"Ask them how they got through their previous most difficult times and listen to what they tell you. They might say, 'We leaned on each other. We reached out to our family. We faced it head-on with honesty.' Whatever the answer is, remind them that is exactly how they will get through the healing and the new normal that lies ahead. And remind them that their new normal also includes never having to worry about breast cancer again."

How have you faced difficult times before? That's a question I often ask people who are facing a terribly painful experience because it reminds them that they have survived terrible pain before, reminds them *how* they survived it, and gives them hope and faith they will survive again.

I gave this young woman a final piece of advice that I have shared in more hospital rooms than I care to remember. I explained that all of us are alive today because we are the descendants of those who came before us. Our very DNA would not exist without them. Those most likely to survive millions of years ago were those who lived as if there was a tiger behind every tree. They survived by imagining the worst and living as if the worst was going to happen. Expecting the worst might have been a useful way of seeing the world millions of years ago. Today it is just the opposite. Pain specialists and psychotherapists call this way of thinking catastrophizing. It is a documented fact that catastrophizing is a greater predictor of decreased quality of life than pain intensity alone is.

Whenever I am troubled and really afraid, I think of the times I have been on a plane, flying through clouds and stormy skies, white-knuckled through the worst of turbulence. Feeling my stomach drop during the most violent dips and bumps, worried that this time the plane just might go down, I remind myself that I need to ride it out, hang on, believe, and remember that there is a beautiful blue sky awaiting me above all that turbulence and fear in my life. I am not suggesting that awful things cannot happen—merely that what will actually happen to us before, during, and after a painful experience is likely to turn out far better than our most fearful imaginings. Catastrophizing is a terrible waste of physical, psychic, and spiritual strength when we need it the most, and believe me, one way or another, whatever outcome you are imagining will be wrong in any case.

"Just keep going."

When people call me to start planning a funeral for someone who is still alive, I remind them not to miss the rest of their loved one's life worrying about and planning his or her death. When you are facing a difficult situation, the less time spent imagining the terrible things that might happen days, weeks, months, or years later, the better. Sure, when standing on the edge of a cliff, we all look down and imagine what it would be like to fall off, tumbling toward the ground with no control to a certain death. But when you are in pain, you must do what you can as often as you can to back yourself away from the cliff's edge and seek a more productive perspective. Keep yourself on a short time leash. Ask, *What can I be doing in the next hour to take care of my loved one, to take care of myself, to make the current situation better, to ease the pain?*

Pain causes depression and depression causes more pain. This is true, by the way, whether the pain is physical or emotional. Both types of pain trigger the same areas in the brain. Believing your pain is going to get better will not cure the pain, but it will lessen it and prevent it from dominating your entire life. Pain specialist Steven Richeimer offers a simple way of summarizing this type of positive psychology: You think about ways to turn each negative fear into something that offers you more positivity and control. For example, change "I just can't take it" to "I can relax to feel better." "It will never go away" to "It waxes and wanes." "It will ruin my life" to "My life can still be full of purpose and meaning." "It will only get worse" to "I can control how much attention I give it." "I have nothing to look forward to" to "There is a lot I can still do and new things I will do that I have never done before." "I will never be happy again" to "There will be many things in the future that will bring me joy." Live with faith in the future and in yourself—one hour at a time.

"Do you want to walk again without a limp and without a cane?" my physical therapist, who worked mostly with wounded veterans, limbless and afraid, asked me at my first session with her after my surgery. "Do you want to walk without a limp?" she asked again. "Then stand up and look into that full-length mirror on the wall." I thought that she was going to show me some technique to correct my limp, some trick to try as I watched myself walk in front of the mirror. Instead, she told me to look at myself—really look at myself. To stare into my own eyes for a very long time.

As I did, she told me that our brains suffer a sort of post-traumatic stress disorder after a painful and extended physical injury just as they do after emotional trauma. Although the source of the pain has been surgically removed and the actual pain has stopped, our brains are expecting more pain and therefore prevent us from using and trusting our bodies fully. The same is true of our hearts after we suffer severe emotional pain. We have been hurt by a spouse, disappointed by a child, cheated in business, lied to by a friend . . . so rather than trusting again, we draw inward to protect our wounds and avoid future trauma.

So often I hear people quote Ernest Hemingway, who said, "The world breaks everyone, and afterward many are strong at the broken places." That has always sounded more like Hemingway bravado than the truth to me. I am sure some people do grow stronger in their broken places, but I know my back isn't stronger and never will be. I know that a broken marriage, a broken heart, a ruined reputation—none of those things grow stronger. But we can heal enough, we can somehow find our true selves again—or for the first time— and what we find really is often gentler and wiser and more beautiful than before. A second love. A second chance. Another way to walk forward.

"Now, remember who you were before this happened. The real you. The inside you," the physical therapist said from across the room. "That man is still there. Wounded, weak, spent, afraid, but that man is there. You must decide whether or not you will fight to find him and to be him again, but wiser, and kinder to your body and yourself. You must decide to trust again—to trust your body again, to trust in the world and its goodness again, to trust in yourself again."

That old expression came back to me then with Zen-like clarity: when you must . . . you can. One hour at a time.

THE PRISONER CANNOT FREE HIMSELF

You are never strong enough that you don't need help.

— Cesar Chavez

There was a famous miracle worker named Yochanan. But when this great man with healing power became ill, he could not heal himself.

His friend Hanina came to visit him. Hanina said to him, "Give me your hand." He took Yochanan's hand and raised him up from his bed.

"Why couldn't Yochanan raise himself?" the old story asks.

"Because," it answers, "the prisoner cannot free himself from prison."

Every one of us sooner or later feels pain—somewhere, deep inside our body or our heart. That person sitting next to you is in pain. That stranger on the subway is in pain. That person who cut you off, who cut you down, who cut you out, is in pain. The people you love are in pain. You are in pain. To love is to grieve. To live is to hurt.

Pain, emotional or physical, reveals our vulnerabilities. It presses where it hurts. We can grimace and ignore that pain. We can blunt it with pills, booze, sex, shopping, eating, vaping, or weed . . . but no one in pain, despite what they might say at the time, does better enduring their pain alone. The better way is to listen to your pain, respect your pain, and talk about it with people who can help you understand its true source. Pain is an invitation to change the depth of conversation. Face pain's truth, pour it out to God or to the people you love. Reach out to the people you love and who love you. Tell them. Trust them. They will hold your hand and raise you from your suffering.

There is an old folk tale about a grieving widower who visits the village wise man for some solace. The wise man gives the mourner a list of ingredients necessary to bake a sweet cake and tells him to go around the village gathering one ingredient from each home. The only requirement is that the ingredients must be from homes never visited by grief or sorrow. At the end of the day, the widower returns to the wise man empty-handed. There was not a single home in the village wherein someone had not suffered a painful loss.

The story is more nuanced than it first appears. Most people assume that what helped the widower was his realization that everyone suffers pain. My guess is that he, like us, already knew that. I think what made the difference was the conversations that likely took place in each home and with each neighbor.

I am so sorry. I cannot give you an ingredient because I too have suffered terrible pain.

What happened? Tell me about her.

Let me tell you about my loss. How much I miss him.

How much I appreciate the wonderful person and gift she was to me.

Tell me more about your fears and sorrow.

Let me share with you how I have managed to go on.

The man's suffering did not end that day, but his healing began. He no longer felt so cursed or alone.

He knew everyone at some time walks through the Valley of Shadows where he too was now traveling. It was the ebb and flow of kindred spirits, fellow sufferers reaching out, sharing, consoling, advising, and caring, that helped pierce the widower's isolation and helped him take the first steps on the path to healing.

Reaching out is not easy for most of us. It is hard for independent, successful, self-sufficient people who are used to helping others to reach out for help themselves when they are suffering. What's more, 80 percent of people with chronic pain suffer from clinical depression, and depression makes people far less likely to reach out for help and less receptive to those who want to help. I know it would have taken years longer for me to make peace with my pain—if I ever would have—without the help of a compassionate and talented psychiatrist and without my friends and family, with whom I was willing to confide my fears.

Sometimes we are afraid we will burden the people we love to the point of alienating them when we need them the most. When I talk with people who are afraid to reach out to their spouse, their kids, their parents, their friends, or their colleagues,

I merely ask them to consider how they would feel if the situation were reversed. What if your sister, your child, your parent, your friend or colleague was suffering and needed help? Wouldn't you want to know? Wouldn't you want to help? "Of course I would" is most often the answer.

You cannot survive terrible pain alone. Trust the people you love enough to tell them you need them, you are afraid, you are confused, you have made a terrible mistake, you have nowhere to turn. You will be amazed by the people—some of whom you had no idea cared so much about you—who, because they too have suffered, feel more keenly your pain. You will be grateful, and in some ways healed, knowing that the people whom you love most love you even more deeply and profoundly than you ever knew, even—especially—when you are broken by life.

Is there risk in reaching out? Will some people disappoint you? Of course. It might seem a little glib to put it this way, but it's very important to remember that when you reach out in pain, the people who really matter don't mind, and the people who mind really don't matter.

Ideally, this means that all of us who have lived through pain and are grateful to those who responded know we too can free others. Ali, a woman left deaf, mute, and half paralyzed from her many cancer surgeries, typed to me in one of our conversations as we passed a laptop back and forth:

> There are angels all around us. Angels in our friends, our family; people we meet. Sometimes you don't see those angels until you really need them. I kept in touch with some of my friends from work, and word got around that I was going to Nashville for treatment. People got together and planned some fund-raising events to help me get through this time and to help with travel expenses. I heard that they had some kind of a bake sale and posted my picture with a little story about my situation in a few places.
>
> I was amazed. I would never ever have thought people cared that much. A co-worker came to my house and gave me a big bag of get-well cards and letters and a check for three thousand dollars. All for me? I couldn't believe it. It was so uplifting to know that I wasn't forgotten.

What about when we are not the victim of suffering, but the witness? What do we do for a person in pain who is our family, our friend, our colleague, our neighbor? What can we do to ease another person's suffering?

One of the great Rabbi Akiva's students became ill, but none of the sages went to visit him except Rabbi Akiva, who swept and cleaned the floor for him. Because he did this, the student recovered.

The student said to him, "Rabbi, you have revived me!"

Then Rabbi Akiva returned to the academy and taught, "Those who do not visit a sick person might just as well have spilled his blood."

Rabbi Akiva understood the importance of reaching out, and Woody Allen was right when he suggested that the single most important thing in life is showing up. Time and time again I hear it from those who are hurting. The simplest gestures matter.

"I have learned many things these last few months," wrote Rabbi Nachum Braverman, after his baby girl Yael was diagnosed with cancer. "All of my friendships were tested in the crucible of those terrible days when we first learned of Yael's illness. I began to value simpler qualities in my friends than

I had previously. Caring seemed more important to me than brilliance, and far more rare.

"At a time when I needed it badly, there were few people who took the time to involve themselves in my life. At first I judged harshly those who didn't come forward until I considered whether I would have behaved differently myself. I realized how often I had failed others through preoccupation with my own talent, which was clearly much less important than the ability to care." This was from an article he wrote many years ago in a now defunct magazine called *Olam*.

One of the things I often tell people who are in the beginning stages of a painful ailment or crisis is that they are gratifyingly about to find out who their friends are, and disappointingly who they are not. A lot of people run away when trouble comes to someone they know. Maybe because they subconsciously fear that the affliction will somehow metastasize to them, or maybe they just don't know what to say or do to help. But in any case, there is no doubt that some people will disappoint you when you are in need and others will surprise you with their ability to show up.

Two of the greatest figures in the Bible are Abraham and Moses. Each of them was called by God and each of them answered the same way, with the Hebrew word *Hineni*—"Here I am." We too are called by our own suffering and the suffering of those around us to reach beyond ourselves, to reach out with the simplest of words—*here I am*.

Week after week I get calls from people asking me what to say to their loved one who is facing the scalpel or chemo or divorce or public shame or so many other types of pain. The truth is, there are no answers to the chaos that is pain. There is nothing to say except "*Hineni*—Here I am." In fact, what you don't say when someone is suffering is even more important than what you do say. I often tell people never to say these seven words: *Let me know if you need anything.* Saying "Let me know if you need anything" puts the burden on the sufferer rather than on us. When my father-in-law died recently, many of the very same people who were in the pews when I preached about never saying "Let me know if you need anything" said just that in e-mails and text messages. "Let me know if you need anything" smacks of false empathy and the hope that the sufferer will not actually respond.

When you visit a sick person, think of what he or she needs most and, if it's in your power, give it. If you are visiting in the hospital, make your visit brief so that you do not exhaust the patient. If the person is mired in the pain of the moment, try taking him or her on a sort of mental vacation back to happier times. I sometimes ask people to tell me about the best vacation they ever had, or to tell me the story of when they met their beloved husband or wife, or their first kiss, or the funniest thing that ever happened to them. A brief escape and a brief reminder of happier times is a welcome and loving gift.

When I visit someone who has received get-well cards in the hospital or at home, the cards from family and friends are usually taped up on the wall or set out on a table. Notes, cards, calls, and visits mean a lot. If someone asks to be left alone for a while, respect it. Otherwise, visit, call, e-mail, visit, call, e-mail, visit, call, and e-mail some more.

It's our job to anticipate the needs of people in pain and meet them without being asked. Help with the obvious things: carpool duty, healthy dinners delivered to their doorstep, playdates for the kids, send a massage therapist to their house, take some of the pressure off at work, go with them to doctors' appointments. Sometimes a little creativity is in order. But whether your friend who is suffering is far away or close to home, most important of all is to listen, and listen bravely. People in pain are worried and they need someone to worry with them. Be willing to listen, no matter how sad it makes you. Listen and be unafraid to talk of death or fear. This is real friendship. This is real love.

Help in less obvious ways too. Ways that restore dignity and hope. A great teacher and writer named Joseph Telushkin tells a beautiful story about his father, Shlomo. Shlomo worked full time as an accountant for one of the world's greatest religious leaders. Suddenly Shlomo was afflicted with a stroke. One day while Shlomo was still in the hospital, his son Joseph received a call from one of the religious leader's top aides, who had an accounting question he wanted Joseph to ask his father. It had been only a few days since his father regained consciousness. He was weak and confused. So Joseph hesitated to ask him the question. The assistant persisted and explained that at a meeting earlier that day, when this accounting question came up, the great leader said, "Ask Shlomo." When the leader was reminded how sick Shlomo was, he repeated, "Ask Shlomo."

Now knowing that the question came directly from the great leader, Joseph went to his father's room and posed it to him. Shlomo offered an immediate response. At that moment Joseph realized the leader's brilliance and compassion. The leader knew how sick Shlomo was, but he also understood how important it was for him, lying in a hospital bed, confused and half paralyzed, to still feel needed.

"All of my friendships were tested
in the crucible of those terrible days."

The greatest deed is to ease the suffering of another, and most people will do just that if given the chance. I know who reached out a hand when my suffering was at its most unsightly. I remember Andy and Dahlia's flowers, and Audrey's, Deborah's, and Geri's too. I remember the e-mails; my friend Bruce, who showed up and installed Apple TV to get me through the long months of recovery. Cindy brought a cushion so that I could sit in a chair with less pain. My physician and friend Jay called every day; so did my consulting physician, Ted. Don and Nancy showed up with dinner, Barbara made me soup, David brought over Stephanie's gooey blonde brownies, Hannah put her arm around me and carried me to the bathroom, and so did Aaron. When I lost my appetite and so much weight, Betsy made me countless grilled-cheese sandwiches—the only thing I wanted to eat for weeks; comfort food in the deepest meaning of the word. Stacy and Alberto sent cupcakes, each with a single letter on top, that together spelled out *Get well soon*. Marilyn sent the most ridiculously delicious ice cream from Cincinnati. Rick made sure the hospital checked me in without waiting. Daniel came over to the house to cut my hair. My nephew Andrew sent me a new iPad to help me with answering e-mails while lying down. Another friend, also named Andrew, who had had similar surgery, called when I was at my lowest just to tell me he knew I was suffering and to promise me that "Everyone gets better." At that moment, however slightly, the clouds began to lift. I remember each fellow sufferer of pain who was willing to listen to my fear that I would never walk again; each gesture of connection and caring.

Both Judaism and Christianity anticipate the future coming of a messiah or a messianic era of redemption for all of humankind. "Where shall we look for the Messiah?" asked the ancient sages.

"Shall the Messiah come to us on clouds of glory, robed in majesty and crowned with light?"

One sage imagines this question posed to no less an authority than the prophet Elijah himself. "Where," the sage asks Elijah, "shall I find the Messiah?"

"At the gate of the city," Elijah replies.

"How shall I recognize him?"

"He sits among the lepers."

"Among the lepers?" cries the sage. "What is he doing there?"

"He changes their bandages," Elijah answers. "He changes them one by one."

Reaching out to those who suffer, one by one, is a holy act.

"On the morning of my final course of treatment," writes Marlene Adler Marks of her battle with lung cancer, "I was ready for the long, seven-hour routine now familiar to me. . . . My portacath was easily accessed. The intravenous drip of steroids and kidney stabilizers was set in motion. [My friends] Emily, Joyce, and I were discussing the career prospects of our adult children. At 2 P.M. the doorway filled; my oncologist and the staff brought a chocolate cake and sang 'Happy Last Chemo to You!' . . .

"At 6 P.M., we caught the mistake. The IV pump had a glitch. . . . For two and one half hours, while Susan, Cynthia, and Rona had been discussing art museums and second careers, I'd been getting nothing from a blocked port.

"And so I was back at the beginning. Not just the beginning of the day, but, my thoughts sent spiraling, the beginning of my life. Fear took over, my blood pressure rising into the stratosphere. And I knew, with a certainty only six months of lung cancer could produce, that this was bad news. My grandmother, who died before I was born, had had high blood pressure, followed by a stroke. She'd gone blind. All my life seemed pointed at this moment, this awful dark joke. My cancer wouldn't kill me, but high blood pressure might.

"'Can you meditate?' nurse Stephanie asked as she turned down the light. . . .

"'Om,' I began. And 'Shalom.'

"I started the slow counting of the breath, in and out. I saw myself on a sandy beach of a tropical island at sunset. I breathed God in, and tried to breathe fear out.

"Nothing worked. The slower I breathed, the worse my fear became. I was the proverbial speck, a victim of a senseless universe, with the terror of my grandmother's legacy whispering in the wind.

"And my blood pressure stayed high.

"Then I heard the rustle of leaves. . . . Susan was there, flipping through the newspaper nearby.

"'Hold my hand?' I asked her. Within minutes, I was breathing normally. My blood pressure had stabilized.

"So on the very last day of chemotherapy, one valve of an IV tube was constricted, but another valve, the valve of the heart, opened up.

"I know nothing about bravery. I know only about need. . . . [about] reaching out, to friends who are close at hand."

AN INTIMATE INVITATION

*When you reach out to those in need,
do not be surprised if the essential
meaning of something occurs.*

— STEPHEN RICHARDS

Consider the famous Bible story about Moses smashing the tablets of the Ten Commandments into bits out of anger and frustration over the Israelites backsliding into paganism and idolatry by worshipping a golden calf. Most of us know how the story ultimately turns out. God forgives, as God usually does, and sends Moses back up the mountain to get a second set of tablets to replace the first shattered set. What most of people don't know is that 2,000 years ago the sages of the Talmud asked a question about that famous Bible story. "What," asked the sages, "happened to the bits and pieces, the rubble and the shards from the first set of tablets? Where did they go?"

The sages go on to claim that the people picked up those shattered pieces and placed them alongside the second, whole set of tablets and placed both the broken and the whole in the sacred ark they carried with them through the desert as they wandered for 40 years. Finally, the sages turn that story into a lesson about how to care for a person who has lost the ability to care for him- or herself; whose life is merely bits and pieces of what it and they used to be.

This story has helped me embrace my father in ways I never could as a child. There was great stress in my childhood home. My father was tough. He ruled the house mostly through fear because his abusive parents were so emotionally damaging to him that he knew no other way. He never hit us, but he was tyrannical and I often thought he might. If my brother or I misbehaved, we might be told to strip down to our underwear and stay in our rooms all day and night; a sort of prison for children. When he saw my older sister reading a book that had a picture of an African American man on the cover, he grabbed it and threw it in the incinerator. Though it took me many years to understand it, my backbreaking work ethic started long ago while I was scrubbing floors on my hands and knees in the workers' locker room at my father's junkyard. I remember him shouting, "All I want to see are asses and elbows!" I was ten years old; my little brother, working alongside me, was eight.

My father isn't tough anymore. We knew something was wrong when he started trying to make phone calls with the TV remote control. He was diagnosed with Alzheimer's soon after. Now he mostly sits asleep in his nursing home wheelchair, wearing a diaper and a bib. My parents had a difficult marriage—always. But I will never forget the way my mother helped my father put on his socks and shoes before the Alzheimer's robbed him of his ability to walk. She had found something within her and within my dad that had been lost for a very long time. It was real and kind and difficult and beautiful. When I visit my dad, I touch him and hold his hand in silence. I scratch his head to make him smile. I kiss him. I forgive him and I tell him again and again and again in ways I never could have before that I love him. I cannot explain this paradox of strength in weakness except to say that when someone we love is vulnerable and in pain, it is an invitation to love them even more.

My wife, Betsy, and I have a magical love and we always did. When we met, I had a part-time job running the Sunday school for a small congregation in Cincinnati. Betsy was a new friend of the school's art teacher and was with her when she came to work that day. The teacher walked Betsy into my tiny fake-wood-paneled office with walls that did not reach to the ceiling and books scattered everywhere to introduce her guest for the day. When my eyes met Betsy's shy gaze and azure eyes . . . everything stopped. We went out for dinner the next night and spent 12 hours sitting by the bank of the Ohio River talking mostly about the pain we had suffered. Her cancer, the treatment for which had ended only weeks before, my painful breakup with another woman, hers with another man . . . Days later, on our second date, we became engaged. Everyone thought we were crazy. We knew better. Last year was our 30th anniversary.

Of course, we have faced many hardships in our marriage. Betsy has rescued me from despair many times. But I do not think I ever loved her more than when she developed dire complications after a recent surgery and was hospitalized for three weeks—so weak and in so much pain. They discharged her from the hospital with drains dangling from her abdomen. Each morning and evening, I emptied the sickening green and yellow fluid into a measuring cup and recorded the data. It might seem surprising, but more than marriage, sex, having children together, or any of the times she cared for me in my infirmity, this was the most loving and intimate thing I have ever done with or for another person—an intimacy and love born of pain and need. To love and care for someone who is whole is one thing. To love and care for a person when he or she is broken, weak, and afraid is quite another. That is the deepest kind of love; a love discovered only through vulnerability and pain.

"This was the most loving and intimate thing I have ever done with or for another person."

One of the most intimate, heartbreaking, and beautiful responses to pain I will always remember began with a phone call.

"Rabbi, do you make house calls?" the man named Mike on the other end of the phone wanted to know. "My dad was never religious, but he said he'd like to see a rabbi before he dies. He's living with us now. He has no place else to go and he can't get out any more. It's cancer. Please?"

The address was up a winding canyon—a winding urban LA canyon—traffic whizzing by, houses packed up against each other like so many kernels on an ear of corn. The front yard was brown and weedy, with a broken sprinkler and a folding chair off to the side. I knocked and Mike let me in.

"Dad, the rabbi is here to talk to you," Mike said loudly over his shoulder. "Go ahead, Rabbi. He's in the living room on the couch."

Mike looked much older than when I last saw him. I had officiated at his wedding some five years before. Now he was gray and balding. He was tired. When I found his father, Bud, on the couch, I knew why. Bud was in the last stages of lung cancer, his skin thin, spotted, and brittle as a dead leaf. His body was mostly bones and his face so gaunt his eyes seemed too large for his head. I sat next to him, yet a universe away, in my navy suit, crisp white shirt, polished shoes, and dimpled tie. Bud, in his diaper, gray sweatpants, and undershirt, with a leakproof pad beneath him, looked at me. He had no idea who I was or why I was there. Although he wasn't in pain, every gesture, every syllable, took more strength than he had to spare. I wanted to help Bud. So in my most compassionate rabbi's voice I said, "Bud, I'm the rabbi. I know you wanted to see me. How can I help?"

Bud slowly rotated his head in my direction, locked in on me with his huge brown eyes, and whispered, "I have to take a crap."

I said I was here to help, I thought to myself, *but there's a limit. You want to talk theology, you want to pray, you want to plan your funeral with me—I'm game. You want me to change your diaper—I'm out.* I went to find Mike. "Uh, I think he has to go to the bathroom," I said timidly. Mike sighed and headed toward the living room. I pulled back to watch a remarkable dance unfold.

"Okay, Dad," Mike said, facing his father on the couch and bending over. "Put your arm around my neck. Come on, Dad. Put it up there. That's right. Come on. Now the other one. Don't let go, Dad."

With Mike's help, Bud managed to put both of his sticklike arms around Mike's neck and lace his fingers together.

"On three, Dad. One, two, three—up we go. That's it. Don't let go," Mike urged Bud as he slowly lifted him off the couch so that they were now face-to-face. Bud's body slumped against Mike's.

His arms were still locked in place behind Mike's neck. Mike's arms were around Bud's waist. Then the dance began—the most tender dance I have ever seen.

"That's it, Dad," Mike encouraged, as he slowly rocked from side to side and Bud shuffled each foot, still grasping Mike with all his strength. Ever so gently, Mike inched them both toward the bedroom, where Bud could lie down and have his diaper changed.

"That's it. Good, Dad. Now I know why Mom said you were such a great dancer." Side to side. Inch by inch. The old man and his middle-aged son, holding on to each other against the sadness and the ache—swaying to a melody only they could hear.

Bud died a week later. When I met with Mike to learn more about his dad before the funeral, I found out why Bud was living with him. Bud was broke. His first wife had thrown him out for losing all their money being suckered into scams. His second wife had thrown him out for the same reason. That's when Bud moved in with Mike.

Bud had a joke for every occasion. He was down and out so often that he had a special place in his heart for anyone in trouble. He couldn't do a favor for you fast enough once you asked him. He was a snappy dresser, loved elephants, could fly a plane, and man, could he dance. Also, Bud could sell anything. In the '70s he was the guy who showed up on your doorstep to sell you a vibrating bed. Just give him a second to set up the demo model in your living room. In the '80s it was shoes. In the '90s, oil well investments. Bud always knew that wealth and power were just around the next corner. All he had to do was mortgage the house to get there.

When Bud was dying, Mike was all he had. Mike was his only child. They shared the same birthday. They had shared the same apartment when Mike was a young boy, and now they shared the same house as Bud was nearing the end of his life. When Mike was young, Bud used to come home late from work some nights, wake Mike up, bounce him in his bed, and toss him in the air. Then "one, two three—up we go," onto the kitchen counter, Mike feeling 10 feet tall, to dip graham crackers in cold milk. Sometimes Bud gave Mike a bath. In the end, Mike had to clean up Bud's messes. There was a beautiful, fearful symmetry to it all. Bud's wives left him. His friends turned out to be crooks. His son's wife wanted Bud in a home. But Mike just hung in there with his dad, picking up the shards and shattered pieces, gathering up the rubble of a life that once was, and placing it in the most holy of arks—his heart.

We all know someone whose life is shattered. The elderly, shattered by age. The lonely, shattered by divorce and loss. The frightened, reduced to rubble by malignant cells gone mad, the accident, the sudden turn of fortune, the fallout from an embarrassing indiscretion. The ancient rabbis knew what to do. Mike knew what to do. All of us know what to do.

We have to hold on to each other. "One, two, three," and up we go, all of us swaying to a melody only we can hear.

PRAYER

Prayer begins at the edge of emptiness.

— ABRAHAM JOSHUA HESCHEL

I don't think praying to God prevents disasters or cures cancer, because I don't think God causes disasters or gives people cancer in the first place. But I do know that prayer unlocks tears and hidden sorrow.

I do not believe in prayers that cure, but I do believe in prayers that heal. When I pray for my father, whose Alzheimer's disease will only get worse until he dies, I am not praying for him to be cured. He won't be. I am praying for my family to heal together as we try to protect and comfort my dad as best we can. For our broken hearts to heal. For the healing that comes when we make peace with that which we cannot change.

Most often when I pray I am not asking *for* something. Instead I am asking to be *rid* of something: to be rid of anger, arrogance, and pettiness; to be rid of everything that keeps me from being my best self. I pray in a way that depends not upon God but upon me. This is true whether I am the one who is suffering and I am praying on my own behalf, or I am witness to others' sadness and I am praying for and with them. Prayer pierces isolation, surrounding us with swaying, songs, and comfort when we pray with others and with peaceful solitude when we are alone. Prayer says to the sufferer on whose behalf we pray, *I care about you. I am thinking about you. You are not suffering alone and unnoticed.* Prayer is hope.

I know the concept of prayer is difficult for those who do not believe in God. When people tell me, as they do often, that they do not believe in God, I always ask them what they *do* believe in. In every case, in thirty years of asking that question, the nonbeliever has gone on to articulate a deep sense of faith in some power defined by a word other than *God*; but a power greater than human beings nonetheless.

Of the rationalist I ask only this: Where is it written that the rational and the spiritual cannot live together in one heart? Where is it written that we must choose science or religion rather than science *and* religion? They ask different questions, they seek different answers. In *Why Faith Matters,* David Wolpe quotes the great scientist Stephen Jay Gould, who put it this way: "Science and religion are different enterprises and serve different purposes in our lives." Wolpe then goes on to paraphrase Gould's view that science is about discovering facts and religion deals with other and perhaps even more important questions about why we are here and the purpose of the cosmos, things about which science has nothing to say.

"For those who believe in God," remarked Francis Collins, director of the Human Genome Project, "there are reasons now to be more in awe, not less."

To say we do not believe in God because we believe in science is like saying we do not believe in love because we believe in math, or to say I cannot love my daughter because I love my son. Religion and science are two different things, neither dependent upon the other for its existence. "I would not treat my cancer with prayer alone and disregard the accumulated wisdom of modern medicine," writes my friend David Wolpe, a cancer survivor, in his book on faith. "Nor would I regard my body as nothing but an animate mesh of gears and wires. I took medicine and prayed; submitted to tests and believed that there is a purpose to things, intelligible and mysterious. Science and spirit are not opposed. They join hands in our lives, often to save them. They did mine."

"Where is it written that the rational and the spiritual cannot live together in one heart?"

When a member of my congregation named Rusty asked to see me, I went to her home, spent a little time with her husband, and then walked with him into her bedroom. Rusty was thin and weak from chemo, a clear, thin tube wrapped behind her ears and under her nose, forcing oxygen into her lungs, her breath shallow and labored, her skin thin and brittle.

"Rabbi, thank you for coming. I'm dying and wanted to see you, but you should know I don't believe in God."

"That's all right," I whispered, holding her hand. "But tell me, Rusty. What do you believe in?"

"Orion and Mother Nature," she answered without hesitation.

"Rusty, do you know what the first verse of the Bible says?" I asked her.

"No."

"It says, 'In the beginning God created the heavens and the earth.' That must have included Orion and Mother Nature. That's what our ancestors meant when they said God created the heavens and the earth. They meant that there was something greater than us and beyond us but which we are all a part of nevertheless and to which we all return. Isn't that what you mean, Rusty—that you believe in the power and the mystery of the universe and your ultimate return to that power, that vastness beyond us all? Rusty, if that's what you mean by Orion and Mother Nature, then you are a believer. The Bible says the very same thing with different words."

"Well, then I suppose I am a believer," Rusty answered before drifting off to sleep.

Everyone who has ever told me he or she does not believe in God believes in something. Orion, or Mother Nature, a Higher Power, science, or at the very least that the sun will rise after the darkness of night. We all believe in the sunrise. We take it, as it were, on faith.

Does it really matter if you call that thing on your wrist a watch or a timepiece? We are all talking about the same thing. Judaism holds that there are seven different names for God that are considered so holy that once written they cannot be erased. Why seven different names? Because there are many paths to the same conclusion. Choose whichever words you wish—Nature, Science, the Cosmos, a Higher Power, the Unified Field Theory, Ruler of the Universe—all of us believe in a force beyond and within us that is greater than our own existence.

Is there a single person on earth who really believes that our destiny is entirely in our own hands, that we are not subject to forces beyond us? When the Bible or Quran or any religious text quotes God saying, "I am God," that text is also saying, ". . . and therefore you are not God." No one of us is God. Only a terribly immature person looks to the stars without humility and wonder. There is something about distance that paradoxically brings clarity. That's one of the things that religion does for us . . . it gives us the long view from above or beyond, fitting our own lives and journeys into a broader, more profound and eternal context. Seen from the heights, our own problems become smaller, and the fact that we are a part of something sweeping and grand becomes impossible to ignore.

The sages who wrote the earliest prayers, these symphonies to God, were surrounded by death and suffering. They lived during a time when it was common for women to die giving birth. There were no cesarean sections in gleaming white hospitals, with an epidural, crushed ice, and a DVD player—instead, they died. The great spiritual figures in history lived during a time when it also frequently happened that a child did not live to see his or her first birthday. No bubblegum-flavored antibiotics for infections—they died. Granted, there was no midlife crisis 2,000 years ago, but only because there was no midlife. You were a child until you were 12 or 13, then you got married, went to work, had children of your own, and by the time you were in your mid-30s, you were most often toothless and, before long, dead. The ancients had to know, just as we know, that all the praying in the world didn't keep people alive; they knew there was no cosmic granter of wishes. That's not why they prayed, and it's not why we ought to pray.

We pray to be aware, to be amazed by life, nature, and love. We pray to demand of ourselves that we be humane human beings and not animals. We pray to thank God, or whatever name other than that you prefer, that power behind all powers; the power of the mountain and the sea, my children's laughter, my wife's shy smile, ripening fruit, and flowers opening petals to the sun; the power of the cosmos and the quark; the power of breath in our souls each morning; the power of awe and wonder. We pray out of gratitude to that God, that force, that power, that miracle, that whatever-word-you-choose, which grants us life itself.

I keep a prayer on small laminated cards in different places all over my house. It's a prayer of gratitude for awakening that day. I say it quietly every morning before leaving my family to begin my day. Because most days a call or an e-mail informs me that someone is dying, or might be dying, from cells gone mad, or the scalpel, or the clot, the plaque, the infection, the "We're really not sure but her vitals are getting worse." I pray every day in gratitude for my body, to remind myself of the terrible pain I suffered and how grateful I am that my pain is so much less and my life so much better in so many ways because of that pain. I pray to remember, as a 40-year-old man with three children who suffered a heart attack once said to me, "Even a bad day is a gift." I pray because someday something will happen to me and I will die. My prayers are of gratitude for every moment until my last.

The great rabbi Milton Steinberg said, as paraphrased by Dennis Prager, "The believer in a moral God must account for one thing, unjust suffering; while the atheist must account for everything else." When pain comes, use whatever name you wish, whatever it is you believe in, and talk to that force, that power, that name. Pour out your fear, your sadness, and your ache. Hold on to that in which you do believe; that which is within and also beyond you. Because in that holding on, you too will be gently held.

THE HOUSE
OF MEMORY

Love is as strong as death.

— SONG OF SONGS

Julie Maude Miller's son Sean died at home. Her friends wanted her to sell her house so that she would not be haunted by memories, so she could let go, move on. This is her story:

> We had been living in the house we built near Idaho's Snake River canyon for eight years when Sean, our fourteen-year-old son, died of cancer on the tapestry sofa upstairs in the family room. We were granted that one small grace—to allow him to slip away from us where he always wanted to be, in the home

that was his sanctuary and ours, witness to our joys and tragedy.

I am proud Sean didn't have to spend his last days in a sterile hospital room hooked up to tubes and machines. Instead, he lived on the sofa, whose fabric he wore thin while he was ill, planted in front of the VCR and television. At home, everything was peaceful and familiar to Sean, the window he looked out of every day, the open stairway that allowed him to hear everything going on downstairs when he was too weak to navigate the steps, the wall of windows through which there were frequent deer sightings—usually when they were ravaging our shrubs in winter, but the deer were welcome to the shrubs because they distracted our little boy.

I look at the kitchen table—the first time we returned from the hospital we were all traumatized by Sean's diagnosis. His 16-year-old brother, Tyler, stayed home from school the next day to play cards with Sean. When Sean's cancer metastasized for the last time, the boys played cards at the same table, the day before Tyler went off to basic training at the Air Force Academy.

Tyler carefully hid behind a mask of quiet strength the fear that he would never see his brother alive again. Sean held on, but when Tyler returned six weeks later, it was just two days before the end. Sean wasn't strong enough to play cards downstairs, but he did manage to walk into the bedroom nearest to his tapestry sofa to play one last card game. My husband and daughter and I lay on the bunk beds and watched, all of us together in that tight space. I would never have thought that watching my boys play cards could be so inexpressibly heartwarming.

The bunk beds are still in the boys' room. If I concentrate I can relive climbing the ladder to the top bunk, where Sean used to sleep before he got sick. After his illness he was afraid of being alone at night, and Haley, our littlest one, was suffering from this first threat to her predictable, loving world, so we clustered futons around our small double bed so the children could sleep in our room. We were grateful to be so close together. It was the only security we had left.

The house holds so many memories. There were summers playing baseball in the meadow, endless hours of shooting baskets, sledding down steep slopes nearby, and the gleefully welcomed snow days—no school because we live on an unplowed road. We filled those snowbound days with homemade cinnamon rolls and board games. Now when I open the kitchen closet door, there are lines and dates marking the children's heights: Tyler's on the left, Haley's on the right, and Sean's in the middle, stopping prematurely when he was 12 and radiation to his thigh bones halted his development. While recording our children's growth, we were measuring time and imagining a future that we never suspected would fall so short of our expectations.

Since we lost Sean, these walls have listened patiently to the tears I held in while Sean was alive, because I knew I couldn't fall apart on him. Only our little house has heard me because I know my grief is safe here. These walls won't try, as friends with good intentions do, to distract me or make me feel better.

Julie knows, she understands, what grief and love are really about. They are not for running away, for distraction, for feeling better or moving on.

They are for settling in, for staying put, for holding on tight to the one thing that we still have—our memories. Pain is permission, space, and time—to just remember. The world, our friends, the self-help books, our colleagues and acquaintances, they all want us to move on, to move out of the house of memories that is the only thing we have left to warm and protect us. The world leaves us so little permission, so little space, so little time just—to remember. Grief takes time—to cry, to hold on, to miss them and ache for them and want them and to hold them in our minds and our hearts without being asked to move on. To remember them before the disease, the dementia, the accident, the CT scans, the doctors, the needles, and the tubes. To remember them smiling, playing, advising, in their favorite sweater, in their favorite chair, at their favorite restaurant. To remember them laughing—just laughing, hard and real with that sparkle in their eyes.

Pain is the house that will listen patiently to your tears. Your grief is safe there. Its walls won't try, as friends with good intentions do, to distract you or make you feel better. They will protect you and hold you while you take your time—to remember.

AN INVITATION
TO BE KIND

The goal for most people should not be
to feel better, but to get better at feeling.

— SHANNON L. ALDER

At a conference not long ago, someone asked me about the book I was working on, and I told him it was about the lessons we learn from pain. He asked me what the result of my own pain was, and without hesitation I said: "I am a nicer person." Not that I was a mean or evil person before, but experiencing pain made me a nicer one. This man then pointed something out to me that I had never thought about before. He pointed out that the Bible says God places words and commandments for kindness and decency upon our hearts.

"Why does God place these words *upon* our hearts? Why not place these holy words *in* our hearts?" he asked me.

Then he answered his own question, quoting a sage:

"It is because as we are, our hearts are closed, and we cannot place the holy words in our hearts. So we place them on top of our hearts. And there they stay until, one day, the heart breaks and the words fall in."

I have never understood how people can pray for mercy and compassion from God but not be merciful and compassionate themselves. Compassion is central to every major religion in the world. In the most famous Jewish example of this, a pagan asked the great Rabbi Hillel to explain all of Judaism to him while standing on one foot—not much time to explain an entire religious tradition. Hillel summarized an entire worldview by saying, "Do not do unto others what is hurtful to you. The rest is commentary. Go and study."

A religion scholar, Karen Armstrong, put it this way: "Every single [religion] has evolved their own version of what's been called the Golden Rule. Sometimes it comes in a positive version—'Always treat all others as you'd like to be treated yourself.' And equally important is the negative version—'Don't do to others what you would not like them to do to you.' Look into your own heart, discover what it is that gives you pain, and then refuse, under any circumstance whatsoever, to inflict that pain on anybody else."

Henry James put it another way: "Three things in human life are important: The first is to be kind. The second is to be kind. And the third is to be kind." Everything else is commentary.

Chris Abani is a Nigerian dissident, author, and storyteller. "What I've come to learn," he says, "is that the world is never saved in grand messianic gestures, but in the simple accumulation of gentle, soft, almost invisible acts of compassion, everyday acts of compassion. . . . During the Biafran war . . . it was my mother with five little children. It takes her one year, through refugee camp after refugee camp, to make her way to an airstrip where we can fly out of the country. At every single refugee camp, she has to face off soldiers who want to take my elder brother, Mark, who was nine, and make him a boy soldier. Can you imagine this five-foot-two woman, standing up to men with guns who want to kill us?

"All through that one year, my mother never cried one time, not once. But when we were in

Lisbon, in the airport, about to fly to England, this woman who saw my mother wearing this dress, which had been washed so many times it was basically see-through, with five really hungry-looking kids, came over and asked her what had happened. And she told this woman. And so this woman emptied out her suitcase and gave all of her clothes to my mother, and to us. . . . That was the only time she cried. And I remember years later, I was writing about my mother, and I asked her, 'Why did you cry then?' And she said, 'You know, you can steel your heart against any kind of trouble, any kind of horror. But the simple act of kindness from a complete stranger will unstitch you.'"

"One day, the heart breaks and the words fall in."

People often sit on my couch of tears to pour out their sorrows, to weep, to ask, "Why?" When it is their marriage that is the source of those tears, the answer to *why* is sometimes very simple. Somewhere in the journey that was their marriage, they just stopped being nice to each other. They just stopped being kind.

Do you want to stay married? Be kind. Do you want to hold on to your kids even when they are adults themselves? Be kind. Do you want to be close to your brothers and sisters? Do you want to have friends? Do you want to be respected and successful in business? Do you want to be proud of who you are—who you really are? Be kind. Research now indicates that we are at our best when we actually do think with our hearts. Scientists have demonstrated that certain chemicals released from the heart are responsible for stimulating the part of our brain that makes compassionate choices. When we are at our best, our most human and humane, we think with our hearts.

My friend Rabbi Ronne Friedman's son Jesse committed suicide a few years ago. Ronne was the cool, hip rabbi at the summer camp I went to as a kid. I became a rabbi in part because I wanted to be like Ronne. Here's a part of the eulogy he gave to honor his own son: "We are brokenhearted. We cannot hide our brokenness. Let me tell you what we know: Each of you would willingly give us a piece of your heart if it would help to make ours whole. We know, we know. For us, that is the only intimation that the laws of gravity might one day be restored."

A piece of our hearts willingly given, the heart of another gratefully received. The ebb and flow of friendship and love, care and kindness. Kindness is the only thing that enables any of us to go on.

Pain is an invitation to those of us who survive the suffering to become kinder, better people. Even more powerfully, pain is an invitation in the midst of our suffering. I have never heard the opportunity for greatness that pain presents put better than in this story about a test of character.

A group of American businesspeople went to Israel and had an audience with Rabbi Nosson Tzvi Finkel, the head of a famous seminary. One of the attendees described the encounter this way:

> Rabbi Finkel was severely afflicted with Parkinson's disease. He sat down at the head of the table, and, naturally, our inclination was to look away. We didn't want to embarrass him. We were all looking away, and we heard this big bang on the table: "Gentlemen, look at me, and look at me right now." Now, his speech affliction was worse than his physical shaking. It was really hard to listen to him and watch him. "I have only a few minutes for you. . . . Who can tell me what the lesson of the Holocaust is?"

He called on one guy who didn't know what to do—it was like being called on in the fifth grade without the answer. And the guy says something benign like, "We will never, ever forget . . ." And the rabbi completely dismisses him. . . . All of us were sort of under the table, looking away—you know, please, not me. He did not call me. I was sweating. He called on another guy who had such a fantastic answer: "We will never, ever again be a victim or bystander."

The rabbi said, "You guys just don't get it. Okay, gentlemen, let me tell you the essence of the human spirit. As you know, during the Holocaust, the people were transported in the worst possible inhumane way by railcar. They thought they were going to a work camp. We all know they were going to a death camp. After hours and hours in this inhumane corral with no light, no bathroom, cold, they arrived at the camps. The doors were swung wide open, and they were blinded by the light. Men were separated from women, mothers from daughters, fathers from sons. They went off to the bunks to sleep. As they went into the area to sleep, only one person was given a blanket for every six. The person who received the blanket, when he went to bed, had to decide, 'Am I going to push the blanket to the five other people who did not get one or am I going to pull it toward myself to stay warm?' . . . It was during this defining moment that we learned the true power of the human spirit, because we pushed the blanket to five others." And with that, he stood up and said, "Take your blanket. Take it back to America and push it to five other people."

ENOUGH
IS ENOUGH

Eighty percent of the world
lives on less than 10 dollars a day.

— **WORLD BANK**

I got out of bed
on two strong legs.
It might have been
otherwise.
I ate
cereal, sweet
milk, ripe, flawless
peach. It might
have been otherwise.
I took the dog uphill
to the birch wood.
All morning I did
the work I love.

At noon I lay down
with my mate. It might
have been otherwise.
We ate dinner together
at a table with silver
candlesticks. It might
have been otherwise.
I slept in a bed
in a room with paintings
on the walls, and
planned another day
just like this day.
But one day, I know,
it will be otherwise.

Jane Kenyon wrote this poem in 1993, upon hearing her husband's cancer diagnosis. Ironically, it was Kenyon, not her husband, who died a year later from a fierce and swift onslaught of leukemia. The "otherwise" she foresaw came unexpectedly one day, with no regard for the silver candlesticks, the paintings, the birch wood, or the flawless peach.

Pain diminishes us, and it is so important to remember, in the midst of pain and everything that pain takes from you, that still . . . you are enough. You are enough just as you are. You are worthy of love and kindness. You are enough. And you have enough.

Whether in our own pain or in witness to another's suffering, life is a miracle for which we ought to be grateful every day, because it could be otherwise.

The Polish psychologist Bluma Zeigarnik proved that when you show people a picture of a circle with a small wedge cut out of it, their eyes first go to the missing piece and miss the much larger whole every time. In the midst of pain and loss, it's hard to recognize how much remains. If you want to change your life—really change—wake up to the blessed life you already have despite your pain.

"Rabbi, in just two more weeks he would have been 90," a son tells me as we prepare for the funeral. "In another year they would have reached their 65th anniversary," says the daughter. I understand their disappointment, but I also remind them that 89 years and 50 weeks of life and 64 years of marriage are full, whole, beautiful, blessings.

Often, when I start to feel sorry for myself because I think life has dealt me some unfair decree, I think about a conversation I had with a friend who is a famous comedy writer. "Whoever said there's no justice is right," he said to me. "Thank God there is no justice. If there was justice, I would be a slave in a factory or bent over in a field someplace like most of the world instead of getting hit over the head with a bag of dimes every time I say something funny."

"I stand in my closet at the end of so many long days, reaching for a hanger, pondering the tear stains on my suit coat from holding someone earlier that day in front of an open grave."

I know what many people think when I encourage them to count their blessings. "Okay. We get it. We're lucky. We're not starving. We're not living in a hovel. But things go wrong in our lives— terribly, painfully wrong." Believe me, I know. I know because it's my phone that rings when a family needs to find a treatment program for an addicted teenager, or wonders if I know of a good family law attorney or a job opening somewhere, anywhere. And I know because I've stood in my closet at the end of so many long days, reaching for a hanger, pondering the tear stains on my suit coat from holding someone earlier that day in front of an open grave.

"Imagine, if you will—a gift," says Stacey Kramer in her TED Talk. "It's not too big—about the size of a golf ball. . . . It's going to do incredible things for you. It will bring all of your family together. You will feel loved and appreciated like never before and reconnect with friends and acquaintances you haven't heard from in years. Adoration and admiration will overwhelm you. It will recalibrate what's most important in your life.

"It will redefine your sense of spirituality and faith. You'll have a new understanding and trust in your body. You'll have unsurpassed vitality and energy. You'll expand your vocabulary, meet new people, and you'll have a healthier lifestyle. And get this—you'll have an eight-week vacation of doing absolutely nothing. You'll eat countless gourmet meals. Flowers will arrive by the truckload. People will say to you, 'You look great. Have you had any work done?' And you'll have a lifetime supply of good drugs.

"You'll be challenged, inspired, motivated, and humbled," Stacey continues. "Your life will have new meaning. Peace, health, serenity, happiness, nirvana. The price? Fifty-five-thousand dollars, and that's an incredible deal. . . . This gift came to me about five months ago. . . . It was a rare gem—a brain tumor, hemangioblastoma—the gift that keeps on giving.

"And while I'm okay now, I wouldn't wish this gift for you. I'm not sure you'd want it. But I wouldn't change my experience. It profoundly altered my life in ways I didn't expect. . . . So the next time you're faced with something that's unexpected, unwanted, and uncertain, consider that it just may be a gift."

Ironically, it's easier to count your blessings when you have cancer or some other terrible challenge than it is when things are fine. Most of us lead pretty ordinary lives most of the time, and that's a challenge in itself, because it's hard to appreciate just how extraordinary *ordinary* really is.

While having breakfast at my hotel the morning after I delivered a speech in Austin, Texas, I happened to sit next to a Texas state assemblyman who had attended the prior evening's presentation. We chatted about this and that and then I asked him what I thought was a common and appropriate question posed to most politicians, which was, "What's the next office you plan to run for?"

"Why do you ask?" he challenged. "Isn't what I'm doing now important enough?"

His response stopped me short. He was so right.

If you ask me to define what it means to be a spiritual person in one sentence, I would say, "It is the sanctification of the ordinary." All religious and folk traditions I know of have some sort of prayer, blessing, or ceremony related to the most mundane aspects of daily life: sharing a meal, seeing the sunrise or the new moon appear, waking up in the morning, eating bread or some other very simple food. Why? Why a blessing over something as ordinary as bread? It's simple of course . . . if we can be grateful for bread, then we can be grateful for the other, greater blessings of life as well. Ideally, we are at our best when we take no small thing for granted. It is a wiser person, a happier person, a more successful person, a better person, who even in pain, or especially in pain, can affirm the enoughness, the beauty, the miracle of bread.

THE ROUTE OF
ALL BLESSINGS

*Even if there were pains in heaven, all who
understand would desire them.*

— C. S. Lewis

Once there was a man who knew nothing about agriculture who came to a farmer to learn about farming. The farmer took him to his field and asked him what he saw. He saw a beautiful piece of land full of grass and pleasing to the eye. Then the visitor stood aghast as the farmer plowed up the grass and turned the beautiful green field into a mass of brown ditches. "Why did you ruin the field?" asked the man.

"Be patient and you will see," answered the farmer.

Then the farmer showed him a sack full of plump kernels of wheat and asked him what he saw. The visitor described the nutritious, inviting grain and then once more watched in shock as the farmer ruined something beautiful. This time he walked up and down the furrows and dropped kernels into the open ground wherever he went, then he covered them up with clods of soil.

> "'Be patient and you will see,'
> answered the farmer."

"Are you insane?" the man asked. "First you destroy the field, then you take this beautiful grain and you throw it underneath."

The farmer answered, "Be patient and you will see."

Time went by, and once more the farmer took his guest out into the field. Now they saw endless straight rows and green stalks sprouting up from all the furrows. The visitor smiled broadly. "I apologize, now I understand what you were doing. You made the field more beautiful than ever; the art of farming is truly marvelous."

"No," said the farmer, "we are not done; you must still be patient." More time went by and the stalks were fully grown. Then the farmer came with a sickle and chopped them all down as his visitor watched openmouthed, seeing how the orderly field became an ugly scene of destruction. The farmer bound the fallen stalks into bundles and decorated the field with them. Later he took the bundles to another area, where he beat and crushed them until they became a mass of straw and loose kernels. Then he separated the kernels from the chaff and piled them up in a huge hill. Always he told his protesting visitor, "Be patient; we are not done."

Then the farmer came with the wagon and piled it high with grain, which he took to the mill. There this beautiful grain was ground into formless choking dust. The visitor complained again, "You have taken beautiful grain and transformed it into dust." Again he was told to be patient.

The farmer put the dust into sacks and took it back home. He took some dust and mixed it with water, while his guest marveled at the foolishness of making whitish mud. Then the farmer fashioned the mud into the shape of a loaf. The visitor saw the perfectly formed loaf and smiled broadly, but his happiness did not last. The farmer lit a fire and put the loaf into the oven.

"Now I know you're insane; after all that work, you burn what you make."

The farmer looked at him and laughed. "Have I not told you to be patient?"

Finally, the farmer opened the oven and took out the freshly baked bread, crisp and brown, with an aroma that made the visitor's mouth water. "Come," the farmer said. He led his guest to the kitchen table, where he cut the bread, and he offered his visitor a delicious buttered slice.

"Now," the farmer said, "now you understand."

Think about the most wonderful and meaningful things in your life, past or present. Next, see if you can trace those good things back to something difficult or painful that gave birth to them. Childbirth itself is an example of a blessing issued forth from pain. A lot of blessings are actually rooted in suffering. For example, falling in love with my wife was the greatest, most magical experience of my life, and it still is. But that falling in love happened only as the result of a broken heart and painful split from my previous girlfriend and my wife deciding to end an equally dysfunctional and painful relationship with her previous boyfriend.

This shared misery in our past helped us to know and understand each other's hearts, and our own. Taking care of my mind and my body in my middle age came only as a result of the pain caused by abuse and neglect in my younger years. Ask someone who appreciates his job why and he will often tell you about a much hated job or boss in his past. Ask someone how she became a successful businesswoman and she will likely tell you about years of harassment, naysayers, and long hours. Ask any great inventor or artist what lead to his or her most moving creation and you will hear a tale of critics, doubters, and painful but instructive failures.

Take a blessing inventory—an accounting of the best things in your life and the best things about you. More times than not, those best things and qualities were forged in the fires of adversity. Remembering where most blessings begin will help you withstand the searing heat of those fires.

Healing

LIKE LOVE, NATURE WILL HEAL YOU

There is something infinitely healing in [the] repeated refrains of nature, the assurance that after night, dawn comes, and spring after the winter.

— RACHEL CARLSON

Joshua Tree National Park in California is where the Colorado and the Mojave deserts come together to create a magical scattering of massive boulders rounded by ceaseless wind and rare desert torrents over millions of years. The brown, tan, greenish, and gray rocks rise above a forest of jagged cactuslike Joshua trees; all of it is set against the bluest of blue skies. I loved to boulder in Joshua Tree. Bouldering is pretty much what it sounds like—find a boulder and climb it. Bloody hands and knees, wedging your toes into a fissure and pushing off while reaching for a small, jutting piece of rock to pull yourself up on, crawling reptile-like on your belly, neck arched toward the sky—whatever it takes for as long as it takes. Aggression, singularity of purpose, force, and fear are all a part of bouldering, and they were all a part of my life in so many other ways too.

As a result of my surgery, I can no longer boulder. Ironically, this has caused me to love Joshua Tree even more. Instead of hiking and climbing with my old aggression, I now walk slowly into the desert and sit on a low, humble boulder that no self-respecting climber would consider—often for hours. As I sit, I see, hear, and feel the desert in ways I never saw, heard, or felt it before. I hear the wind from far away rumbling through a distant canyon long before I feel that same wind on my face. My body, still, is warmed in the sun. I notice like never before the lime green, red, brown, and gray lichen flora encrusting the rocks, glowing like a 1970s psychedelic black-light poster. I hear my own breath and then I hear nothing, nothing but the wind. . . . And then I pray in a way I never prayed before my surgery.

I used to have to work at prayer, chase after prayer. Now, in the sitting, the floating, the dwelling with nature, the prayer comes to me. God comes to me from afar and from within. To be in nature is to surrender to our smallness, our stillness, our oneness with creation, becoming a part of something larger and more beautiful than our own immediate suffering.

"To be in nature is to surrender to our smallness."

There is a rhythm and power to nature. It is greater than any one person's sorrows, even when that person is you. Seeing the warm red and honey-yellow speckled leaves before they turn brittle and brown, knowing that they will soon fall to earth and nourish the next generation of the lush forest floor, is a sermon about beauty and worth at every stage of our lives, and one that frames death as a necessity for life itself. Noticing how the wind-driven sands have smoothed the edges of a boulder over millions of years is a lesson in the brevity of our lives and the small part we play in the great drama of existence, no matter how long or short by human standards our lives might be. Nature's cycles and transformations from death to life and life to death pulsate through all of existence, independent of our personal anxieties and worries. To see our pain in the grand sweep of nature is to know that we were neither singled out for suffering nor granted immunity from it—we are all merely and beautifully a part of the flowing rhythm that all things obey. Nature is proof that life can never really be destroyed, that the urge to grow is irrepressible. Nature gives us perspective and hope. Perspective and hope are the beginning of healing.

This was true even in Auschwitz. "One evening," writes Viktor Frankl in his book *Man's Search for Meaning*, "when we were already resting on the floor of our hut, dead tired, soup bowls in hand, a fellow prisoner rushed in and asked us to run out to the assembly grounds and see the wonderful sunset.

"Standing outside we saw sinister clouds glowing in the west and the whole sky alive with clouds of ever-changing shapes and colors, from steel blue to blood red. The desolate grey mud huts provided a sharp contrast, while the puddles on the muddy ground reflected the glowing sky.

"Then, after minutes of moving silence, one prisoner said to another, 'How beautiful the world could be!'"

I AM SO SORRY

*Most people behave badly when wounded.
If you can remember the wounds, it is far
more possible to forgive the behavior.*

— JONATHAN SAFRAN FOER

I learned about the case of Joe Kay more than a decade ago, and I still think about it a lot. Since I never followed high school basketball in my own state, let alone a neighboring one, I had no idea that Kay was one of the best players in Arizona, in addition to being a brilliant student, musician, and humanitarian. I also had no idea what happened to him at the end of a certain game.

Sports Illustrated explained it this way:

> It's the night of Feb. 6, 2004. Joe Kay is the 6"5', 175-pound flagpole whose monster dunk

has just put Tucson High up for good against archrival and state powerhouse Salpointe. . . .

The buzzer sounds, the rafter-scratching crowd of 1,000 spills onto the floor as if a dike has burst. A throng of delirious boys runs madly at Joe Kay. . . . They are coming too hard. He tries to brace himself, but two guys flat-out tackle him. A dozen more pile on. Joe Kay gets twisted [and] winds up in a hospital; his right side is paralyzed. . . . "This is big, this is permanent, and this is devastating," the doctor said. . . .

"There's no why about it," says Joe Kay, who walks and talks and thinks with a little hitch now. "It just [happened]. It sucks. It happened to me. I don't dwell on it. What are you going to do about it? I mean, how bad is it compared with what's happening to people in Sudan? In India?"

At the time the article was written, it had been a year and a half since his injury and there was only one thing Joe wondered. He wondered when the two guys who tackled him would say they were sorry. "I mean, I know they didn't mean to hurt me," he said, "I don't want to sue them. But it's kind of upsetting. I just think they should apologize. I think everybody would feel better."

I met with a class of second-graders one morning and told them that although they were only in second grade and far from taking the SAT, they already knew the hardest vocabulary words in the English language: *I'm sorry. Please forgive me. Apology accepted.*

Consider the old joke about the chairman of a multinational corporation who every year before the annual shareholder's meeting would gather his corporate board together along with his family and friends, put them all in a room, and say to them, "If I've done or said anything at all this past year to offend you or hurt your feelings, I just want to say, you're too sensitive!" Why is it so hard to apologize when we have caused another person pain?

One reason is that we live in a society that punishes people for apologizing. Doctors are a prime example. One doctor fighting for tort reform put it this way: "Any 'I'm sorry' can be used to blame the doctor, and that has driven a wedge between doctors and patients. Doctors today are told to shut up and fight if anything at all goes wrong."

So many of us, even if we're not at risk of a lawsuit, take the "shut up and fight if anything goes wrong" approach—with our spouses, our brothers and sisters, our children, our friends. In an unforgiving society, an unforgiving marriage, an unforgiving family—as in our unforgiving legal system—we fear we'll be punished for saying, "I'm sorry. Please forgive me."

But guess what? Thirty-six states have found an answer. They have passed what are known as no-fault apology laws that enable physicians to apologize for mistakes without the apology being admissible to be used against them in court. Two years after Colorado passed a no-fault apology law, only one lawsuit had resulted from 148 apology encounters between doctors and patients. As one attorney put it, "If a doctor can be up-front and decent, and his dealing with patients heartfelt and genuine, that's enough for a lot of people."

Most people just want a sincere "I'm sorry. Please forgive me." And with no-fault apology laws in place, doctors are willing to say it. Imagine if we had a no-fault apology law in our families. Imagine the peace and reconciliation possible if we all—parents and children, brothers and sisters, husbands and wives, friends and business partners—made it safe to say, "I'm sorry. I made a mistake. Please forgive me." And imagine the peace and reconciliation possible if we were then willing to accept those sincere apologies. Do we really prefer to nurse our anger, withholding forgiveness even when it is sincerely sought? Must we keep open the option of pulling old grievances off the shelf long after they have been apologized for, only to hurl them again and again at the people we say we love? Or do we want to take the approach encouraged by Jesus's disciple Matthew when he says: "So if you are offering your gift at the altar and there remember that your brother has something against you, leave your gift there before the altar and go. First be reconciled to your brother, and then come and offer your gift" (Matthew 5:23–24).

When I officiate at wedding ceremonies, I say things that are unique to each couple, but there is also something I tell every single one of them. I tell them that almost everything comes and goes in a marriage. Jobs come and go; apartments, condos, and houses come and go; money comes and goes; health comes and goes; the world changes; our bodies change; even our children, just as surely as they come into our lives, leave us in some fundamental way (as the parents of the bride and groom are so bittersweetly aware) as they begin their own marriages and families. Almost everything comes and goes in a marriage. But if one thing remains, then their marriage will thrive and bring them the deepest kind of fulfillment and love. That one thing is friendship, and real friendship depends almost entirely on their capacity for forgiveness. Being able to say and to mean the words "I forgive you and I love you" is love's greatest challenge and greatest gift.

My high school friend Neal's grandfather had a simple way of summing up forgiveness that I will always remember. He put it this way: "What was was, what is is, and that's that." Imagine if we all had families where we could be satisfied with that—where we could say, "I'm sorry. I made a mistake. Please forgive me," and it would really, truly end there. Apology accepted.

If you are a religious person, you know God gets it. If we are truly repentant, as far as God is concerned, what was was, what is is, and that's that. God forgives. But do we? Or do we think forgiveness is only God's affair? "Ah," I sometimes hear back from those who have been deeply hurt by a loved one, "but Rabbi, you don't know what she did! Don't you realize how he betrayed me? Have you any idea how malicious and vicious she is? Do you know what he said? Do you know what she claimed? This forgiveness stuff is all well and good,

But you have no idea, Rabbi. I cannot and I will not forgive."

To this I can only respond, "What about you? Are you so perfect? Have you never slammed a door in anger or shot a hurtful word like an arrow from your lips? Have you never wounded another you claimed to love? How can you come before God or another human being seeking that which you are unwilling to grant another?"

"Whose sin is forgiven?" ask the sages. "The sin of the one who forgives a sin committed against him." Yes, the person seeking our forgiveness must be truly sorry and truly committed to never repeating the sin, but if that's the case, we are obligated to forgive. To forgive mind you, but not to forget. Where is it written that you must forget? Forgiveness does not ask of us amnesia. No one expects forgiveness to eliminate the memory of the offense. But it can diminish the pain.

One sage explained that sin is like pounding nails into a wooden chest. Repentance and forgiveness are like pulling the nails out. The nail may be removed but the hole remains. Forgiveness does not undo the past, but it does make a different future possible.

My friend's sister Ali taught me a lot about letting go of anger. Ali was a beautiful airline stewardess who loved her life of travel—packing snow boots and a bikini for the same trip because she could find herself in Alaska one day and Hawaii the next. All of that stopped when she was diagnosed with a rare cancer of the nasopharynx, which is the area behind your nose and at the top of your throat. Bouts of cancer surgeries and radiation left Ali unable to speak, hear, or eat. She had a tracheotomy in order to breathe and was paralyzed on the right side of her face.

I visited Ali every week or so for more than a year as her health declined. We communicated by passing a lap top back a forth. There was something very deliberate, delicate, and powerful about communicating that way. I would type and pass the laptop to Ali, then wait. She would take a deep breath through her trach, and I would listen to the click of keys while she wrote back to me. Then I would read what she wrote, think, wait, and write back with the clicking keys completely silent to her. The lap top was passed like an offering from me to Ali, then Ali to me. Type, pass, wait, receive, read, type, pass, wait, receive, read, type, pass, wait . . .

We talked about many aspects of pain, suffering, fighting to live, and why even paralyzed and silent, without eating or music, life mattered. We were working on a book of our conversations together before she died at the age of 46 after suffering a stroke undergoing yet another surgery.

"Anger is a lot of work."

During one of our laptop chats, I asked Ali if she was angry about being deaf, mute, and partially paralyzed. Here's what she wrote:

"Yes, I get angry. I don't like being treated like a child just because I can't speak or hear. I hate what has happened to me. But I do not stay angry because it is so difficult to express anger without words. It's much easier to express love. All I have to do is smile . . . and look at my friend or my sister . . . all I have to do is hold her hand or put my arm around her, or laugh when we're talking. I can easily mouth, "I love you," with no voice . . . and the feeling comes through; you don't really need a voice for that. But anger is different. Anger is a lot of work."

Could it be that what Ali was teaching—she who was without words or sound—was that we are better suited, more naturally inclined, better meant to express love rather than anger? Could it be that we were not really meant to punish each other for our mistakes and our angry words, that our future can be different than our past, that we can pull out the nails, forgive, open our palms and hearts wide so that love does not die?

We can remove the nails that have pierced our family and our friendships. Because forgiveness is not only about the past for which we are responsible, but about the future as well. We are responsible for the future of our family and our friendships. Pull out the nails that have torn you and your loved ones apart. Pull out the nails. Because without forgiveness, love dies.

Is there any better lesson, any greater gift, anything more healing than the power of a sincere apology to someone we have wounded? *I am so sorry* unlocks a heart bound up in anger and lights the path to healing for all who suffer pain.

HURT AND RUN

The ability of a person to atone has always been the most remarkable of human features.

— LEON URIS

In the space of one year, two families at the Temple had loved ones killed while they were walking across the street. One, Andrew, had recently graduated from film school and was celebrating with friends who were in town for Christmas week. Before he went out that night, he gave his father a big hug and said, "I love you, Dad." A few hours later, he was hit by a car and the driver kept on going. Eventually the driver, a woman who worked not far from Andrew's parents' home, was identified and stood trial. This is what Andrew's father said to the judge at the sentencing hearing:

Your Honor, I speak today as a dad. Thirteen months ago a police officer came to our house and said, "Your son was found in a roadway and he's been transported to UCLA medical center."

We went to the hospital and a lady came out and said, "Well, your son is brain-dead." That was the way it was conveyed to us.

Over the next four days we prayed with our friends, we hoped for the best, and we held, ultimately, the broken body of our son when he died. And when I say broken body, I mean a child who had part of his skull removed and bones protruding from his leg. He had been annihilated by a three-ton vehicle. And I thought to myself over and over again through this grief, *how are we going to go on as a family?*

The image of my son with tubes in his throat, lying on that bed, and all of his friends streaming through saying goodbye, not being shy, not sparing themselves the pain of seeing such a horror, had a profound effect on me.

We buried our son. We had a lovely memorial service. We had perhaps 1,500 of his friends there and they kept us afloat.

When you talk about a hit and run, you're talking about leaving someone like roadkill, to be run over by the next truck, the next car. You ask yourself what kind of person is capable of leaving a broken body on the highway and driving away, and then going back home, switching cars, and driving back to work. What kind of person works four blocks from where I live and continues to see our pain through the newspapers every day?

Finally, the police get a tip. They go to a house and find a car that's been painted. I know the court has a transcript where the defendants didn't know that they were being recorded at the police station. The wife, the primary defendant in this case, here's what she says to her husband: "Just lie about everything. Don't say anything. Don't admit anything. Just lie about everything."

Detective Skaggs says, "If we continue with this charade, you'll both be in jail. I'm going to get your phone records in about a week. That's going to tell me where you were and where your husband was, and when I show you on the road where Andrew was hit I'm going to put you in jail and he's going to jail for helping you lie."

The wife: "I don't know. I don't know nothing about that."

Detective Skaggs: "You need to do the right thing."

"I have nothing to say. I have nothing to tell. I don't know what happened. How can I tell you?"

Detective Skaggs: "Because you were driving."

"I drove the red car to work that day." She doesn't just deny it. She lies again about the car.

Detective Skaggs: "When you go to prison, do you want the bottom bunk or the top bunk?" And the transcriber writes that she starts snickering.

I want to believe in the best. Early on in the press I said, "If you come forward, I will do my best to understand. It might tear my heart out, but I will try." And I meant that. I understand that people can become frightened and make mistakes. I also said, "If you

don't do that, I will feel just the opposite."
And that's the way I feel today. Just the opposite. These people had an opportunity every
day of the week for months to do the right
thing. People say sentencing will bring our
family closure. It won't. Every day is just pain
management. That's what it is.

Emotional pain management, every day. That's
what this woman left behind for Andrew's family
when she hit and ran.

In the second case that year involving the death
of a Temple family's loved one, the perpetrator,
Karen, made a different choice. She explains the
accident this way:

I am 50 years old and a mother of three
children 19, 16, 8. I wrote a children's book
used in schools all over the country. My husband is a television producer. I have lobbied in
Washington, shaken the hand of our senator,
walked the red carpet at the Golden Globes,
and heard my children chanting Torah. You
can say I had a perfect life. The only problem
with perfection is that it's not.

I was driving with my son in the car and
waiting for a call back about a playdate. The

phone fell off the center console onto the floor. This had happened before, but on this day I wasn't lucky. I reached down to get it and with the phone in my hand I saw a man making his way in the crosswalk—he was doing what he was supposed to be doing—I was not. I had two thoughts as his body flew to the ground. "God, please let him be okay." And, "My life is over."

Bill was 83 years old. Fractured hip, fractured spine, fractured skull, fractured shoulder, fractured wrist, internal bleeding. I called the hospital every day, but I couldn't see him or send flowers. I wasn't welcome. All I could do was cry and pray. I called the traffic officer and said, "I can't stand it any longer. I have to say I am sorry." Five minutes later he called back and said, "William just passed away—you better get yourself a lawyer." My lawyer said there was a real possibility I could go to jail.

Bill's widow told the judge she did not want a mother of three to go to jail, so I received 360 hours of community service. I gave speeches to kids about the dangers of texting and driving. I cleaned up the beach three times a week, eight hours a day, for months, and I walked those beaches alongside other people who had broken the law. Tax evaders, drug users, shoplifters. I cleaned toilets. I picked up things so ugly I cannot mention. I understood the idea of physical labor as punishment and the penance gave me a place to put my anxiety I carried around every day.

It was the people at the beach cleanup that really made a difference for me. Homeless Joe who washed his hair every day in the fountain to create some sort of dignity for himself. Suki who was arrested for drug possession but was building a website to sell her jewelry designs and Sholanda who cleaned a toilet better than anyone else I've ever seen in my life. Up to that point I saw myself in the eyes of Bill's family—a monster. But finally, I saw myself as fallible, as human.

By this time the Jewish Day of Atonement, called *Yom Kippur*, was coming. I was panicked to sit in the Temple and face God. I had committed murder. I felt like God's finger was pointed at me saying "You!"

I didn't know what to do. So I drove to my childhood home in Encino—the cul-de-sac of my youth. I turned the motor off and started sobbing uncontrollably; my fingers were trembling, my ears ringing. I felt like God was witnessing me. I felt exposed. I hit a human being. I took a life. I opened the car door and stood in front of my childhood home where the essence of me was created and said out loud, "I stand before you, God. Here is my plea from my chest."

"I said out loud, 'I stand before you, God. Here is my plea from my chest.'"

I went to the cemetery. I was shaking in the bumpy grass near the grave. I spoke to Bill and I asked for forgiveness. In her book *Sacred Therapy*, Estelle Frankel writes that the sound of the shofar [the ram's horn blown to end the holy Day of Atonement] is like the grieving of a person dedicated to fixing their ways . . . that was me on Yom Kippur.

Something happened to me while sitting in the Temple [on Yom Kippur]. I noticed four words that I never really paid attention to before: *May God bless you.* Simple really, that God could bless me, me the woman who hit Bill. Even though I committed this terrible act, I could still be blessed. . . . I could be good, and if I could be good, then maybe I could accept the love and support of my family and friends, and if I could accept that love and support, maybe I could be lovable, and if I was lovable, I could start to love myself and learn to forgive myself.

In addition to her criminal and civil penalties, Karen chose to do something the courts did not require. I learned about it when Bill's widow, Helen—a Holocaust survivor and Temple member— called me.

"Rabbi, the woman who hit Bill has asked if she could meet with me and our son, Bobby, to seek forgiveness. I don't want to, Rabbi, but if you tell me I should, I will."

"You should."

"I knew that was what you would say. Will you be there with me?"

"I will."

Helen, Bobby, and I met a week before the meeting with Karen. I wanted to prepare them by teaching them something about how repentance and forgiveness really work in Jewish law. The greatest rabbi of all, Moses Maimonides—the Rambam—distilled it down to four steps. If we go through these four steps with sincerity, the result is forgiveness.

First, stop. Stop whatever destructive action you are engaged in. If you are losing your temper with others, stop. If you text and drive, stop. If you gossip, stop. If you cheat, stop.

Second, feel true regret for your error. Feel guilty. Feel the sadness that comes from being something other than your best self. Be sorry for the hurt and the harm you caused. When visited by guilt, do not avoid the pain of that guilt. Face it. Feel it.

Next, confess your wrong and seek forgiveness out loud. This doesn't have to be done at a synagogue, church, or mosque, but it has to be done. Talk to God out loud, not just in your head. Tell God that you are sorry for whatever you did wrong. Then, you must go to the person you hurt and say the three most difficult words for most of us to say out loud: "I was wrong." Say it out loud to your friend, your wife, your husband, your kids, your parents, the stranger, and the Judge of Judges—say it. "I was wrong." Because saying "I was wrong" changes everything.

Finally, make a plan. Figure out a way to make sure that the mistake won't happen again. Put the phone in the glove compartment. Get into treatment for the addiction, seek therapy for your family dysfunction. Pay a self-imposed fine every time you gossip or say something unkind. Whatever your sin, make a plan not to repeat it. The completion of these steps is called "complete return."

I taught Helen and Bobby one more thing. That according to Jewish law, when a person like Karen, who sincerely went through all four steps, seeks forgiveness and is refused three times, she is no longer accountable for her sin. The person who will not accept a sincere apology is the one considered sinful for bearing a grudge.

Karen arrived looking so frail and afraid on the day of the meeting. She spoke first. "I wasn't allowed to speak to you until after the trial. Now that it's all over, I want you to know how sorry I am for what I did to Bill, to your family. It was my fault. I was wrong, and I have tried my best to do everything right since that terrible day, but I know that will never bring him back to you. I am so, so sorry, and I beg you to forgive me."

Bobby, a big, bearded teddy bear of a man, spoke next. "Can I ask you a question?" he wanted to know. "How's your son? He looked so afraid the day of the accident."

"He's okay. Not the same. But okay."

"Can I give you a hug?" Bobby offered.

As he stood Karen fell sobbing into his huge arms. Helen stood and moved toward Karen. She cupped Karen's face in her hands, she kissed Karen's tear-drenched cheeks, and she said: "God bless you." It was powerful. It was beautiful. It was . . . over. Helen called me the next day to say it was the first time in three years she slept through the night.

Long ago I learned as a writer, a son, a father, a husband, a rabbi, a man, that the most important things are said with the fewest words. *I love you. I'm here. No. Yes. It's a deal. He's gone. It's a girl. I was wrong.* The difference between these two accidents is the difference between a few simple words. "Just lie. Lie about everything," and "I was wrong." *Just lie* leaves searing pain management every day. *I was wrong* heals.

Few people, if any, reading this book will likely ever hit and run. That's true. But we all hurt and run. We've all left someone's feelings behind like roadkill. Can we be big enough, brave enough, and honest enough as we stand before the Judge of Judges, ourselves, and those we love to say "I was wrong"? Can you say it? Can you say it out loud to end the heartbreak in your broken friendship, your bitter business, your troubled marriage? Can we say it out loud, we brothers and sisters who do not speak, we parents and children who wound each other over and over and over again; we who hurt and run?

"I was wrong." Look into each other's tear-filled eyes and say it. Hold each other. Heal each other. And may God bless you.

STOOP LOW

The only wisdom we can hope to acquire
is the wisdom of humility: humility is endless.

— T. S. Eliot

A simple folktale written by the sages long ago observes, "A treasury mints many coins with one stamp, all of them the same. But the Holy One minted every person and not one of them is the same. For this reason, every single person must say, 'The world was created for me.'" And every person is to carry that phrase around in his or her pocket as a reminder of each person's unique potential for greatness.

It is true that such a folktale exists and that "the world was created for me" is an authentic way of seeing ourselves and our place in the cosmos. But that is only one-half of the story, and as the old saying goes, "A half-truth is a whole lie." The whole truth is that believing only that "the world was created for me" is narcissistic and arrogant. No good will come of it. Ambition, self-confidence, and faith in our power as human beings are helpful only when balanced with an equal measure of humility; and there is nothing more humbling than great psychological or physical pain. When life falls apart, an arrogant person asks, "Why me?" A humble person asks, "Why not me?" Who do you suppose has the easier time facing their suffering?

It is the goal of pious Christians to imitate the humility of Christ, who was a mere carpenter, rode a donkey, washed the feet of his disciples, and said, "I am among you as one who serves" (Luke 22:27). The Quran reminds us that "The [true] servants of [God] the Most Gracious are those who walk on the earth in humility, and when the ignorant address them, reply with [words of] peace" (25:63).

Abraham, who is, of course, the father not only of Judaism but also of Christianity and Islam because both are rooted in the religion of the ancient Israelites and the Hebrew Bible, says something quite different from "The world was created for me." Instead, Abraham says of himself, "I am but dust and ash" (Genesis 18:27). The very same sages who require us to carry the phrase *The world was created for me* in one pocket also instruct us to place that phrase of Abraham's, *I am but dust and ash*, in our other pocket. This is the ideal way the sages imagined a person should go through life; balancing the impulse to be overly self-important with the impulse to be overly humble and vice versa.

And what of the other great figure in the Hebrew Bible—the greatest of them all, Moses? The final verses of the Pentateuch say: "Never again did there arise in Israel a prophet like Moses . . . for all the great might and awesome power that Moses displayed before all Israel" (Deuteronomy 34:10, 12). Great might and awesome power. That was Moses. But from whence did his power come? Why did God choose him? Because, as the Bible puts it when we first meet him, "Moses was a very humble man, more humble than anyone else on the face of the earth" (Numbers 12:3). There is great power, the greatest power, in humility.

Of course, humility is difficult to achieve. It often comes as a result of terrible embarrassment and pain; it comes at the expense of pride. Consider a certain minister who was admired and loved by his parishioners. After an article appeared about him in the local paper, the minister received a beautiful note from a woman in his congregation complimenting him on his preaching and comparing him with the great prophets of the Bible. She finished by writing, "I think you are one of the greatest preachers of all time."

Feeling good about the note, this minister took it to his wife and asked, "Sweetheart, how many great preachers do you suppose there actually are in the ministry?"

She looked down at the card, looked up at her husband, and replied, "One less than you think, dear."

In his commencement address at Wellesley High School in 2012, English teacher David McCullough, Jr., told the graduates:

> None of you is special. You are not special. You are not exceptional. Contrary to what your soccer trophy suggests, your glowing seventh-grade report card, despite every assurance of a certain corpulent purple dinosaur, that nice Mister Rogers, and your batty Aunt Sylvia, no matter how often your maternal caped crusader has swooped in to save you . . . you're nothing special. . . .

Even if you're one in a million, on a planet of 6.8 billion that means there are nearly 7,000 people just like you. . . .Your planet, I'll remind you, is not the center of its solar system, your solar system is not the center of its galaxy, your galaxy is not the center of the universe. In fact, astrophysicists assure us the universe has no center; therefore, you cannot be it.

This wasn't the first speech in human history reminding us that we are not the center of the universe. God gave that speech to Job 2,500 years ago. To paraphrase the great scholar of religion and mythology, Joseph Campbell, God behaves outrageously in the book of Job. He makes a bet with the devil that he can abuse this good man named Job and this good man will never turn away from God. God takes away Job's wealth, his business, his family, his health, everything. Job's friends say, "You must have been bad."

Job says, "No, I have not. In fact, I have been faithful to God." Finally, Job challenges God. "I'm a good person, God. Why me?"

God shows himself. Does God say, "Look, I made this bet and you have done just fine"? Does God try to justify Himself? No. God says, "Are you big? I am. Could you fill Leviathan's nose with harpoons? I did. Can you keep the ocean waves within the shore? Do you make the sun rise? Try it." In other words, "Who is little man with his puny powers of thought and reason and judgment to challenge the universe to be righteous as a human would be, to attribute human qualities to the universe? The universe is a mystery and I am it."

"I make it rain where no man lives," God reminds Job. Humankind is not God's only concern. Only a fool would think otherwise. It is as if God is telling Job, "Be humble, know your place, if you wish to be wise and at peace with the universe."

To which Job replies, "I have heard Thee and now I behold Thee." He renounces his human judgment in the face of the mystery that is God and the universe.

I have often told my congregation that every single one of them, all human beings, have a divine spark of greatness within; that each of us is great, each of us unique, and the entire world was created for our sake. I say that, and then I remind them to get over themselves because they are nothing more than the blink of history's eye—a speck.

The wisdom, the power, the depth of human experience holds that two contrary beliefs can both be right. That is why we have two pockets. To remind each one of us to live both as if we are great and as if we are nothing. "The world was created for me. I am but dust and ash." It is the dichotomous tension between these two points of view that leads to true wisdom and the ability to face pain without feeling singled out or cursed. Neither the person who is totally egocentric nor the person who is consumed with self-doubt will have a successful life. We need both pockets.

The domes of the world's great cathedrals, the towering sequoias, the soaring mountains and vast oceans should inspire and uplift us. But they should also make us feel small. We are at our best when we are both exalted and brought low. So doubt yourself. Doubt that your side of the story is the only side. Doubt that your perspective is the only perspective. Doubt is so important. "Abolish all doubt, and what's left is not faith, but absolute, heartless conviction," says author Lesley Hazleton, who wrote a biography of Muhammad. "No matter whether they claim to be Christians, Jews, or Muslims, militant extremists are none of the above. They're a cult all their own. . . . This isn't faith. It's

fanaticism, and we have to stop confusing the two."
Great power without humility is not greatness. It is
Hitler, Stalin, Mao, Bin Laden, Assad. It is the belittling boss, the criminal, the abusive parent, the
cold, indifferent spouse.

Do you want to heal the painful wounds in your
friendships and family? Then inject some doubt
into your self-righteousness. Only doubt enables us
to consider, *Maybe it's me. Maybe she is right. Maybe
he does have a point. Maybe I was unkind. Maybe I was
too severe, insecure, self-righteous, proud, or aggressive.
Maybe I was wrong.*

"The words *foolish* and *pride* are often
fused together for good reason."

I am named for my great-uncle who was killed
in WWII, and my Hebrew name includes within
it my parents' names: *Shalom the son of Ariyeh and
BatSheva.* All Hebrew names include both child and
parent. My very name helps me remember my parents, who both fled homes of poverty and abuse,
married at 17 and 18 and had five children before
they were 30. I was raised in a working-class family

where right and wrong mattered, where hard work mattered, where honesty and fairness mattered, where patriotism mattered. And when I am at a crossroads in the desert and wondering which way to go, I remember where I came from and I choose the road of hard work and honesty. The mistakes in my life are always, always mistakes of arrogance. Mistakes I make because I have forgotten where I came from, forgotten the pain that has brought me low in the past, and therefore not been as humble as I should. If we are humble, we are aware of our own faults. If we are humble, we cannot but forgive those same faults in others.

The words *foolish* and *pride* are often fused together for good reason. Pride—believing only that the world was created for you—brings so much foolishness, hatred, violence, and pain to the world and to your life. Only doubt and humility born of pain will heal you. Only doubt and humility born of pain make forgiveness possible. Without them, friendships and families die. I see it all the time. Business partners in litigation, brothers and sisters, parents and children who do not speak, friendships of so many years blown apart. One of the saddest days of my life was when I had to attend an arbitration between my family and my uncle in the midst of my father's worsening Alzheimer's and the sign on the conference room door read *Leder vs. Leder.*

Why must it come to that? Why must it take a tumor, an addicted child, financial ruin, public embarrassment—some tragedy of Job-like proportions—to humble us? Because some of us are not willing to reach deep enough into the pocket of humility that says, *I am but dust and ash. I am no more special than you. I am not perfect. I am not the center of the universe. I am not without flaws and fault, foolishness and doubt.* Wisdom born of pain is the result of reaching deeply into that pocket. Pain is about that pocket.

There is a reason that most religious traditions include some form of bowing, kneeling, or prostration. To be brought low is to remember not only that the world was created for us but that we are dust and ash, that we are prideful, foolish, hurtful, arrogant, dismissive, wrong; that humility before God and our loved ones is the only hope for love to survive.

There is a beautiful Chassidic story quoted by the great Swiss psychiatrist and psychotherapist who founded analytical psychology, Carl Jung. It was Jung who said, "There is no coming to consciousness without pain." According to the story, a rabbi's disciple came to him and said, "In the olden days there were those who saw the face of God. Why don't they anymore?"

The rabbi replied, "Because nowadays no one can stoop low enough."

ABRACADABRA

Words have magic. Spells and curses.
Some of them, the best of them,
once said change everything.

— NORA ROBERTS

The modern day magician's incantation *Abra-cadabra* is a 2,000-year-old phrase in Aramaic—the language Jesus and the great religious sages of the Middle East spoke twenty centuries ago. At the time it sounded more like *Avra kehdabra*. *Avra kehdabra* means "I will create as I speak."

The ancients saw no difference between words and things. In fact, in Hebrew the word for *word* and the word for *thing* is the same—*davar*. Words were considered no different than physical objects; to the ancients words were as concrete and real as anything they could see or touch. They believed very deeply in the power of words. That's why they imagined God in the beginning of the Bible using words to create the universe. God creates by speaking. "In the beginning . . . God said, 'Let there be light,' and there was light." God said, and then there was—*avra kehdabra*. I have always understood this view of language not as a piece of incorrect scientific history but as a lesson to us all, a powerful reminder that we create worlds, we shed light, we destroy worlds, we spread darkness— with words. *Avra kehdabra*—we really do create as we speak.

Think of all the pain we create with words: gossip, slander, insult, derision, false promises, sniping, belittling, coarseness . . . all done with words. So much pain caused by one of our smallest but most powerful muscles—the tongue. A muscle so dangerous the sages say it should be locked behind two gates, our lips and our teeth. Oh the damage we do, the darkness we create, the trouble we get ourselves into, the hurt we cause—*avra kehdabra*—because of what we create when we speak.

The famous Talmudic sage Rabban Gamliel told his disciple Tobi to go to the market and bring back the best cut of meat he could find. Tobi obeyed and brought back slices of tongue. The next day, Gamliel ordered Tobi to go to the market and bring back the worst cut of meat he could find. Again Tobi returned with slices of tongue. Gamliel was confused. Tobi explained, "There's nothing worse than gossip and evil speech. And nothing better than kind and beautiful words." If words can destroy us and the people we love, if words can hurt, then it must also be true that words can heal.

Try this experiment recommended for depression by psychologist Martin Seligman. He calls it a Gratitude Visit. Seligman asks his subjects to close their eyes and remember someone who did something enormously important that changed their lives in a good way, and who they never properly thanked. The person has to be alive. Think of someone who really changed your life for the better. I hope all of us have such a person.

Now consider the homework Seligman assigns. The assignment is to write a 300-word testimonial to that person, then call him or her on the phone and ask if you can visit, but don't say why. Show up at the door, then read your testimonial. According to Seligman, everyone weeps when this happens. When Seligman tests both the visitor and the person visited one week later, a month later, and three months later, they are both happier.

An agnostic named A. J. Jacobs decided to take one year of his life and do something crazy, ridiculous, and fascinating. He decided to live the Bible. He called this experiment and the book that followed *The Year of Living Biblically.* In addition to being hilarious—with accounts of Jacobs herding sheep in Central Park and throwing stones at a 70-year-old friend who he knew was having an affair—Jacobs's year of living biblically taught him some serious lessons too. One of which was, as he put it, *Thou shalt give thanks.* "This one was a big lesson," Jacobs recalls, "because I was praying, giving these prayers of thanksgiving, which was odd for an agnostic. But I was saying thanks, all the time, every day, and I started to change my perspective. And I started to realize the hundreds of little things that go right every day, that I didn't even notice, that I took for granted, as opposed to focusing on the three or four that went wrong."

Most people think we say thank you because we are grateful for something, but in fact, saying thank you actually enhances or even creates our sense of gratitude. Saying thank you leads to greater gratitude, more so than great gratitude leads to saying thank you. This is a testament to the power of words to actually reframe our perspective on our lives and our problems.

"It might sound silly,
but to this day I remember it."

I am far from the first person to point out that whoever said "Sticks and stones may break my bones but words can never hurt me" was wrong. I learned the painful power of words many years ago when I was seven years old. That summer, I won the Best Camper award at Camp Teko—a day camp in Minnesota. Out of all the campers, I was chosen. But when they announced my name and I walked up to receive the coveted trophy from the camp director, I heard only one thing in the midst of my proudest childhood moment. Not my parents shouting with joy or my counselors applauding, but the taunt that followed me throughout most of my childhood: "Little Leder, Little Leder, Little Leder." At the very moment I was being recognized for trying the hardest, the other kids reminded me that I was shortest. It might sound silly, but to this day I remember it.

The pain of a broken bone or scraped knee eventually evaporates from our childhood memories, but never the pain of an insult. Ask any kid who was too heavy, too short, too smart, too tall, or too anything. Words hurt. But of course, if words can cause such terrible, indelible pain, words can also soothe and cure our deepest hurts.

Dr. Laura Trice is a therapist and author who works with people fighting addictions. She has concluded that often people's core wound that leads to addiction is the fact that they never heard the words they wanted and needed to hear from the people who claimed to love them most—namely, their parents, spouse, siblings, or children. People afraid to ask and people afraid to tell others what they need and want to hear are often the unhappiest of all people. So Trice challenges her patients to do something similar to what a bike repair shop does when your tire is not rolling smoothly, something called "truing" the wheel. Each spoke is carefully adjusted back to its original place and tension, and once the entire wheel is trued, the ride is so much better. This is equally true with people. We need to look, ask, and listen, and then to speak the words our loved ones want and need to hear. So Trice encourages her patients to be really honest about the praise they need to hear. "What do you need to hear?" she challenges. "Go home to your wife—go ask her, what does she need? Go home to your husband—what does he need? Go home and ask those questions, and then help the people around you."

Maybe the most gripping and sad reminder I know about the power of words to create or soothe suffering was relayed by the conductor of the Boston Philharmonic, Ben Zander. It's the story of a woman who had been in Auschwitz, one of the rare survivors. She went to Auschwitz when she was 15, her brother was 8, and her parents were lost. This is what she said to Zander:

"We were in the train going to Auschwitz and I looked down and saw that my brother's shoes were missing. And I said, 'Why are you so stupid? Can't you keep your things together, for goodness' sake?' The way an elder sister might speak to a younger brother."

Zander continues the story: "Unfortunately, it was the last thing she ever said to him, because she never saw him again. He did not survive. And so when she came out of Auschwitz she made a vow. She told me this, 'I walked out of Auschwitz into life and I made a vow. And the vow was, *I will never say anything that couldn't stand as the last thing I ever say.*'"

I often hear it said of someone that he was a wonderful person because he always said thank you to people like waiters, parking valets, and store clerks. I actually think that's the easy part. Thanking strangers for a job well done is easy compared with telling the people closest to us that they matter, that we are grateful to them and proud of them. We rarely lose our temper or gnash our teeth when a stranger asks us a question, but we often feel stressed and tempted to lash out at family. It's not easy to be sure that whatever we say can stand as the last thing we ever say.

Pain leaves behind many scars and a few precious opportunities to change, to grow, and to love more deeply. Pain helped me to say thank you more often and more sincerely. Thank you to the members of my congregation for caring about their faith and their Temple and for being so good to me and to my family. Thank you to my gifted, compassionate, and tireless physicians. Thank you to my extraordinary wife, Betsy, for all those dinners, errands, and chores, for all those nights and weekends I could not be there to help, for believing in me, sharing life with me, for filling our home and my heart with such profound beauty and being there through all those fearful moments when pain tested my faith, when I was weak, in tears, depressed, and afraid. Thank you to my children, Aaron and Hannah, for helping carry me when I could not carry them and for being such great kids who I am proud of every day.

Who helped you through your pain? To whom are you grateful? Do they know? Have you told him? Have you told her? *Avra kehdabra*—we create as we speak. Let your pain bring forth healing words of gratitude and love.

LIFE IS LONG

*You musn't confuse [a] single
failure with a final defeat.*

— F. Scott Fitzgerald

I bump into a couple named Ronna and Erik in the lobby at the gym. They are smiling, chatting, and normal. I am glad to see them together and seemingly happy because I know the backstory. "It's really good to see you together after what you've been through," I tell them.

Ronna and Erik's son Harry died at eight years old of adrenoleukodystrophy, a disease made known to many by the movie *Lorenzo's Oil*. This terrible affliction essentially causes a young child to go mad, to lose his own sense of self in every way until he dies. This is part of the eulogy I wrote for Harry, which I am sharing with Ronna and Erik's permission:

It has rained every day since the dark night Harry died. It is as if the entire world has been crying, cold and dark. And in the midst of that dark, cold quiet—in the midst of the world's tears, I am struggling to find the words.

Just as there are no words for love, there are no words for death. There is only pain, and darkness, and sorrow. There is the silence of peering deeply into the power of life, and love, and loss. We feel that power this morning—the power of life, and love, and loss— and it is frightening. We know and Harry's family knows there are no words to say; instead, we offer our silent presence—we are here because we love them. They know that.

There are no answers this morning to our questions—Why Harry? Why this precious, sweet boy? Why such a capricious, rare, and devastating disease? Why now? But this much I do know and I do believe. This anger and fear, this sorrow and suffering is ours, not Harry's. Harry is beyond sorrow and suffering. Harry is beyond the doctors, anxiety, and fear.

The ancient rabbis said that death, even at its worst, is only "perfect sleep." Harry is at rest. Harry is at peace. And we can all, at least, be grateful today for the end of his suffering; for the rest and the peace that Harry so much deserved. Somehow now we too must make peace with his death—at least enough to live. We cannot die because children die.

Harry would agree with that as much or more than anyone, because he loved life with a joie de vivre beyond what most of us will ever know. Harry was a fearless, happy soul who loved to laugh from his belly, even at his own jokes that no one else understood. He had an amazing sense of style. There was his bandana phase, his jewelry phase, his formal-attire phase when he insisted on coming to dinner by candlelight each night in a suit and tie. Harry always just seemed to know what was right for Harry with a sort of inner truth and certitude that most adults could envy but never really achieve. How many kids after scoring a goal in soccer run up and down the field blowing kisses to the adoring crowd? At Harry's core was a deeply embedded sense of joy and creativity, intelligence and inner strength of being, charisma and charm.

Harry loved food, and he was smart enough to usually wind up getting what he wanted. "If I had two moms," he used to say, "the other one would give me candy." At eight years old, Harry had already developed a habit usually reserved for Jewish and Italian men in their 70s. At breakfast he wanted to know what was for lunch, at lunch he wanted to know what was for dinner, and at dinner he started wondering about breakfast the next day.

"Who do you love?" Ronna would ask Harry.

"Daddy"' was always his answer, because he knew the result would be Ronna chasing after him for a kiss. Harry loved Erik, Ronna, and his brother, Sam, with all of his large and generous heart. It was always the four of them and it will always be the four of them at the center of their lives. Harry loved a party. He loved to dance and to play. Harry loved a crowd. He loved to put on a show. And Harry loved something else too—women. He loved to girl-watch at the park, on the playground, and especially on that last, incredible family trip to Bora Bora. Harry was, shall we say, impressed with the fact that women went topless on the beaches there. "Hey, Mom," he asked Ronna, "what's the name of that country where these women are from?"

"France," she answered.

"I want to go there," Harry said emphatically.

One of the last times Harry had a moment of real lucidity, when he put all the pieces together again for just a minute, was his last birthday. For most of the day, Harry didn't really know it was his birthday or why there were presents and people around. But then when the cake came out and the candles were lit, Harry smiled. "It's my birthday," he exclaimed. "Let's dance. Everyone dance with me. All of us together." And Harry had everyone there, the people who loved him and whom he loved most in the world, start dancing. He would accept nothing less than pure joy. That was Harry.

No, we cannot die because children die. We can only live, as Harry in his finest moments taught us to live. Young as he was, he came to teach the profound truth that to grasp the meaning of life, we simply need to hold the people we love. As Erik, Ronna, and Sam gently held Harry, we will hold them. We will hold each other until the rain ceases and the sun warms us back to life and to love.

As I left Ronna and Erik at the gym, I thought about how brief Harry's life was. Then I immediately thought of a friend of mine I used to see at the same gym who died years ago of cancer, a psychiatrist with a wife and two young daughters. I remembered how sad I was on my way home from my psychiatrist friend's funeral. I turned the radio off in the car because I needed quiet. I needed to be alone. I needed to think. I'm not used to burying people my own age. It cuts close to home. It hurts. It wakes me up to the simplest and most terrible truth.

During that sad ride home from the cemetery, feeling numb on the freeway, the same heavy truth I felt after Harry's funeral—that one, cruel cliché—weighed upon me. *Life is short*, I kept repeating in my mind. *Life is short*.

Slowly, the melancholy of the funeral and the drive home lifted. There were a few errands to run, and my kids made me laugh that afternoon. By that evening I felt alive again as I arrived at my now dead and buried friend's home for a brief prayer service. In my blue funeral suit, crisp white shirt, and appropriate tie—not too somber, not too flashy—I put on my rabbinic game face and walked through the door. I scanned the crowd for my dead friend's wife—now his widow—an odd term for a 40-year-old woman with a warm smile and generous heart. There she was, surrounded by her daughters, one of whom was going to have her bat mitzvah in a few days despite her father's death. When he knew he was not going to make it, he asked me to read the bat mitzvah speech he had written for her on his behalf.

Somehow the bat mitzvah happened. There were tears of pain and of pride. A different mantra began to play in my mind, different from the earlier lament on the freeway. *How wonderful it is*, I think to myself, *that life is long*. Long enough for my friend's wife to heal. Long enough for their children to grow and find their own joy again. Long enough for his loved ones to experience whole new lives of another 40 or 50 or even 60 years.

As I leave Ronna and Erik at the gym, as I think of Harry, as I think about my friend and his wife, who is now happily remarried, and his daughters, who have become confident young women, I consider the words of the Israeli poet David Shahar, who once said in an interview, "Where there is no paradox, there is no life." I am caught between two realities, both easy to prove yet diametrically opposed. Life is short. Life is long. Time really does fly at a bewildering speed, and yet life for most people has never been longer in all of human history. Life expectancy in America has doubled in the past 100 years. So which is it? Which truth shall we construct our lives upon—*life is short*, or *life is long*?

Consider the elderly Mr. Johannsen, arrested for trespassing and called before a judge.

"Mr. Johannsen, you have been charged with trespassing on the farmer's property. How do you plead?"

"Not guilty, Your Honor!"

"Mr. Johannsen, you were caught in your boxer shorts, in the farmer's pond, doing the backstroke directly in front of the sign that clearly said 'Private. No Swimming.' Now, how do you plead?"

"Not guilty," Mr. Johannsen insisted once again. "Your Honor," he continued, "I'm not guilty because that's not what the sign said."

"Really?" the judge challenged. "Just exactly what did the sign say then?"

"The sign said, 'Private? No. Swimming!'"

"The most truthful and helpful words . . .
that anyone ever said to me were,
'It will not always be this bad.'"

You see, it's all a matter of emphasis. When we are in pain, the right thing to emphasize is clear. In pain, it is so important to remember that although there are tragic examples of life being far too short, for most of us, life is longer than it has ever been in all of human history, and therefore long enough to heal from our pain. Two-thirds of all the men and women who have ever lived past the age of 65 in the entire history of the world are alive today. For most of us, despite the cliché—despite the frantic pace at which we choose to live our lives—life is long. Remembering that life is long is especially important when we are confronted by the more rare but sad and very painful truth that life is also sometimes far too short.

"I learned that when people described their feelings as 'painful' it was not a metaphor," writes social worker Mary Semel about the death of her son. "I felt pain beyond anything I could possibly have imagined: pain so searing it raised goose bumps on my arms, made me nauseous, left me panting and wondering how soon I could die so I wouldn't have to feel it anymore. I learned that I could live, work, and love in spite of excruciating pain. And what's more, a lot of very ordinary-looking people are out there, more than I ever suspected, who also live with extraordinary wounds. Time and care do temper the pain. . . . The most truthful and helpful words . . . that anyone ever said to me were, 'It will not always be this bad.'

"The pain does lessen; our eyes do stop weeping. Like a watercolor wash, time does soften our suffering. We laugh again. We enjoy our work, our family, our friends. We move on . . . because we know we must. Otherwise, our time here is wasted."

Believe me, I am not campaigning for it, nor does the job exist, but if there was such a job as Chief Rabbi of Those Who Suffer, and I held that job, here is what I would say to the victims of pain. I would remind them that life is long. Long enough to start again, to rebuild, to take more pictures, to create more memories, to heal. I would remind them that the day begins at midnight, the darkest hour, because it helps to live with faith that darkness will somehow be followed by light. I would remind them that hope begins when the moon is new, in its darkest phase, just a slim crescent of light against the black sky. And I would remind them that faith in that which we cannot see through our tears is the truest faith of all.

Have faith that the moon will soon enough be full, reflecting the sun's great power for warmth and light. Believe that there is a time for everything. A time to weep and a time to laugh. A time to remember that there is time enough to heal. Albert Camus put it this way: "In the depths of winter, I finally learned that within me there lay an invincible summer."

The heart monitor, the CT scan, the pink slip, the downtick. There is time; life is long; this too shall pass. Your career is not what you had hoped. You have made a terrible mistake. You have lost your reputation. Your marriage is shattered. Life is long; you can reinvent and redefine. "It is never too late," George Eliot is said to have written, "to be what you might have been." Life is long; we can find our way back to love and meaning if we remain people of faith—faith in our capacity to become what we might have been and faith in the power of time to heal.

I know the overwhelming, cold, dark sea of pain that sometimes engulfs us all. I have traveled that sea myself and with so many others. I know. But I also know the human spirit endures. Life is long; long enough for us to warm slowly, but surely, back to laughter and love. Of this we can be certain and in this we can place our faith. The sun rises no matter how dark the night.

Growing

EXAMINE
YOUR LIFE

The only real conflict you will ever have in your life won't be with others, but with yourself.

— SHANNON L. ALDER

Pain means something is wrong in your life. "If you are visited by pain," warns the Talmud, "examine your conduct." It took the kind of pain that forced me to my knees for me to examine mine. Most of my life, most of the time, I had been able to will myself to outperform ordinary expectations. I believed I was in near total control of my own destiny and body. There was little I thought I could not accomplish if I just worked hard enough. I ridiculed as self-indulgent the daily exerciser and meditator, as weak anyone who took time to lessen the stress of his or her life and work. Had they no ambition, no commitment, no guts? This was my belittling, tyrannical father planted deep within my psyche. It took that backbreaking pain that forced me to the floor to make a change. Now I know the gym, meditation, a walk, a stretch, to breathe in and out, in and out, in and out in quiet and concentration, to sleep, to pull back, to trust others, to enjoy my family, to be alone on a trail, to bike feeling the wind and free like a child again—these are not the self-indulgent luxuries of the frivolous or the weak. These are the fuel of life itself.

Many years ago I gave a sermon that angered a lot of people, and women in particular. It was based on an idea articulated by a friend of mine in one of his sermons. The thesis was that no one can be great at more than one thing. We can be good at many things but we can be great at only one thing. In other words, I cannot be a great rabbi and a great family man. I can be a good rabbi and a great family man, or a good family man and a great rabbi. I have to choose.

This idea struck a very raw nerve in a lot of people, especially women of my generation who were told they could have it all—great career, great family life, great fulfillment—all of it and all at the same time. By the way, men were fed the same lie. The truth is, greatness requires the kind of sacrifice that breaks most people sooner or later, one way or another. In my role I see the family life behind some of the world's most "successful" people. Sometimes it is beautiful, but most times not. The expression "Pretty from afar, but far from pretty" comes to mind. Often the single-mindedness—the punishing drive it takes to be wildly successful—eventually destroys something precious inside people who pay that terrible price.

Of course, when you have a serious legal problem, or a dangerous health problem, you don't just want a good lawyer or a good physician—you want the best, the greatest. A neurosurgeon once said this to me in so many words. People come to him not because he is good but because he has worked and sacrificed to become great, and being great means he can save lives that other surgeons cannot.

He was anxious and tired, and who knows what was happening inside his heart, his soul, and his family. I asked him if at this point in his life he could remain a great surgeon without regret or bitterness, and whether or not he really had to continue at his current work pace. Could he have one office instead of two, for example? Could he turn over the cases another surgeon really could handle with equal results? How much of his stress was of his own making, his own ego, his own fear of weakness? He stopped short, as if I had pointed to something in him he felt but could not articulate.

"Workaholism is the last acceptable 'ism' in many people's lives. I know I was very proud of mine."

If I asked for every alcoholic, gambling addict, drug addict, or sex addict to stand up in church or temple or a football stadium, no one would. Because rightly or wrongly, we view these addictions as character flaws and definitely nothing to stand up for. But if I asked every workaholic in church or temple or a stadium to stand, many of us would stand up proudly, and if we were reluctant, many of us have spouses who would force us to stand. Workaholism is the last acceptable "ism" in many people's lives. I know I was very proud of mine.

More than 800 years ago, the physician and philosopher Maimonides addressed the question of how there could be so much suffering in the world if there is a just and loving God. He identified three different sources of suffering that he makes very clear have nothing to do with God and everything to do with us.

The first source of suffering Maimonides identifies is unavoidable and can be seen as something much less terrible than it seems if properly understood in the context of what it means to be human. A great deal of the suffering people feel when they age is the result of the simple fact that we are human beings made of animate blood, flesh, and bone. Everything changes in nature. Everything declines. You don't like your stretch marks, your wrinkles, your aches, your bad back, or your sore knee, then don't be human, be a rock or a chair. To be human is to fall apart—some of us sooner, some of us later, but we all fall apart. If we are alive and can act upon nature, then nature will act upon us too. That is not an unfair decree from above. That does not make us cursed. It merely makes us human.

The second source of suffering Maimonides describes is the evil that one human being does to another. This too, in his view, has nothing to do with God and everything to do with people denying what is best and most beautiful in human nature. He also points out that most people in most places are not running around harming and killing others. This is true in our time as well. Despite what you would believe from watching the news, most of the world and most of its people are at peace most of the time.

Maimonides then moves on to the final and most predominant source of suffering in the world, a type of suffering that can often be avoided if we are wise and mature enough to recognize its presence in our lives. It is a source of pain and misery most of us know all too well: the suffering born of excess. We eat too much, we drink too much, we work too much, we want too much. If we have copper, we want silver. If we have silver, we want gold. If we have gold, we want diamonds. And we pay a terrible, painful price for the stress and the emptiness that pursuit creates.

Maimonides goes on to point out the genius of nature and the foolishness of humankind. Nature, he observes, provides in the greatest abundance that which human beings need the most. For example, the two things humans need most for survival, air and water, are among the most common and accessible things in nature. On the other hand, the things that are more or most rare in nature—precious gems, for example—are the things we need the least. A lot of us spend most of our time working to make enough money to buy the things that are the most costly because they are the most rare, and yet ironically, these rare and costly things are the things we need the least.

Even when we do stop to count our blessings, we often count the wrong things. Two thousand years ago, the Talmud reminded us that to be rich is to be satisfied with what we have already accomplished. Over five decades ago, Robert Kennedy said GDP "measures everything . . . except that which makes life worthwhile." My Yiddish-speaking grandmother put it another way: "A burial shroud," she quipped, "has no pockets."

We live in a society that would have us believe that we are special; that we are immune from what it means to be made of finite matter—skin stretched over muscle, fat, organs, and blood that all weaken and wound and suffer from abuse and neglect. We live in a culture where being open, being on, and being available 24/7 is viewed as admirable.

Thanks to Dan Brown, the author of the book *Inferno*, and the film of the same name directed by Ron Howard and starring Tom Hanks, many people know about the Vasari Corridor. This private passageway was created for Cosimo de' Medici, the powerful Duke of Florence from the city's most powerful family, to walk from his old palace, Palazzo Vecchio, and his office on one side of the river Arno, over the famous Ponte Vecchio bridge to his new and even more enormous Palazzo Pitti and Boboli Gardens on the other side of the river. Inside much of the secret passageway today hangs a collection of artists' self-portraits. One in particular strikes me as most sad. It's an unfinished self-portrait by the portrait painter Pompeo Batoni, who died in 1787. His nephews found it among his personal items after he died and donated it to the museum. The reason I find this particular self-portrait so sad is that it is unfinished. Batoni, like many of us, worked so hard painting portraits for others that he had little time or inspiration left to make complete and beautiful the portrait and the life that mattered most—his own.

When you are visited by pain, let that pain bring new perspective and new priorities, new respect and more time for your body and your soul. Let it bring new wisdom that says, "Find meaning, purpose, and sustenance in your work—but do not confuse it with your life."

HEADSTONES

With the awakening of his emotions,
his first perception was a sense of futility,
a dull ache at the utter grayness of his life.

— F. SCOTT FITZGERALD

What if you knew you were going to die—not in decades or years, but in weeks, days, or minutes? What is it like to know that this week or day or moment is your last?

Ric Elias was one of the passengers on the plane that crash-landed in the Hudson River on January 15, 2009. He described the sound of the engine going "clack, clack, clack" as the cabin filled with smoke, and he could not help but see the worried look on the flight attendants' faces. From his seat it was obvious the pilot had quickly turned the plane around, lined it up with the Hudson River, and turned off the engines. Finally, he heard him utter three words from the cockpit without emotion: "Brace for impact."

Most people know that because of pilot Chesley Burnett "Sully" Sullenberger III's extraordinary skill, everyone survived the risky water landing on the Hudson. But his near-death experience taught Elias three very important lessons about life. The first was that he needed to stop waiting to be with the people he cared about more often and to do the things he longed to do in life. The second was the realization that like many of us, he had wasted a lot of time in his life on negativity and doing things that did not really matter with people who did not really matter to him. As a result he decided to "Eliminate negative energy from my life. It's not perfect, but it's a lot better. I've not had a fight with my wife in two years. It feels great. I no longer try to be right; I choose to be happy." The third he learned as the mental clock was ticking in his head while plunging toward the water was the absolute centrality of his family in his life. At that moment he believed would be his last, he wished only to be able to see his children grow up.

"About a month later, I was at a performance by my daughter," says Elias, ". . . and I'm bawling, I'm crying, like a little kid. And it made all the sense in the world to me. I realized at that point, by connecting those two dots, that the only thing that matters in my life is being a great dad. . . . I was given the gift of . . . not dying that day. I was given another gift, which was to be able to see into the future and come back and live differently. . . ."

"I realized at that point, by connecting those two dots, that the only thing that matters in my life is being a great dad."

At some level all of us are afraid to die. Religion itself is a response to finitude; to the simple fact that each of us will someday die, and to the desire for our deaths and therefore our lives to have meaning. We all imagine our own deaths, our own funerals, and our own grieving loved ones too. I have held the hands of hundreds of dying people, and that experience has taught me that when it is actually time for most people to die, they are not afraid in the least. Death comes to most people at the end of a long life or a long illness, both of which prepare them and their loved ones for what is beyond. In the holding of those hundreds of hands, when they are actually close to the moment of death, not one person has been afraid. Generally speaking, if you are afraid of dying, it is not your day to die. Anxiety is for the living.

A friend whose 30-year-old son recently died told me, "When people said, 'I can't imagine what it is like to lose a child,' it annoyed me. Every parent has imagined exactly that. Maybe it's the first terrible flu or fall, maybe it's when they are long past due and a ringing phone pierces the night. But every parent has imagined the worst." We all imagine the immense, crushing grief of a dead child, spouse, parent, or friend. For many of us, no imagination is required. We have already walked through the Valley of the Shadows and lowered a loved one's body into the dark, silent ground. Death crushes us . . . at least for a while.

Many religious traditions have rituals and holy days that are meant to mimic death and encourage us to contemplate our own deaths. Fasting, for example, is a form of self-denial that mimics death. These rituals and holy days conjure the future reality that we will die in order for us to take more seriously the ways in which we live. Whether anticipated or sudden, pain and fear that force us to imagine our own deaths, despite how frightening it can be to do so, can change our lives in very positive and important ways.

I have sat with a thousand or more families in preparation for a funeral. It's mostly the small, intimate remembrances of marriage, parenting, and grandparenting that come prominently to life after a person's death. The person's résumé, business accomplishments, awards, or net worth are usually only discussed for a brief moment or two. Death, like pain, strips away the inconsequential. That's why Ric Elias had such clarity as his plane was plummeting toward the Hudson River and why he was bawling at his daughter's play. In facing death he realized that "the only thing that matters in my life is being a great dad."

I am reminded of what matters most in our lives when I walk through a cemetery, which I do often, and notice the extraordinary degree of commonality among headstone inscriptions. Sure, there are the exceptions, my favorite being that of the comedian Rodney Dangerfield, whose headstone says, *There goes the neighborhood!* But generally speaking, when we are forced to encapsulate a person's legacy in no more than a few words, those few words almost always come down to *Loving husband, father, grandfather, and friend* or *Loving wife, mother, grandmother, and friend.*

My childhood rabbi in Minneapolis put it so beautifully when he delivered his final sermon to the congregation on the occasion of his 90th birthday. He began by telling the congregation this sermon would be his last and that he was not afraid to die. And then he simply said:

"Let's look at one another. Let's look at one another each day as if it were the last time. No matter how much we may have looked in the past, it is never enough. Let's look at each other. Let's touch each other. Let's cherish each other's presence, each moment we are together—husband and wife, parent and child, brother, sister, and friend. Let's look at each other with new wonder, new feeling, new love. Let's look at and love each other more."

The ancients could not imagine an airplane plummeting toward earth, but they suffered pain and worried about death as much as if not more than we. They suffered the death of the people they loved and created rituals to mimic death in order to value their own lives even more. They understood, as do we all sooner or later, that death has much to teach us about how we live our lives. So use that fear, that pain, the inevitable truths that death reveals to us the living; use them as a teacher and a friend. Use them to learn and to remember amid the hurry and the worry and the scurry of our everyday lives to look, to really look, at each other. To realize how wonderful it is just to be, and to know, and to laugh, and to love.

BE
UNCOMFORTABLE

*If you're comfortable, it's a sure sign
you are doing things wrong.*

— PETER DRUCKER

Search Google for two particular words and you
will find more than 347,000,000 answers. The two
wonderful words that so many of us spend our lives
searching for are simply these: *most comfortable.*
There are 347,000,000 "most comfortable" products
that can be yours: the most comfortable shoes,
most comfortable chair, most comfortable car seat,
airline seat, dog bed, headphones, underwear, or
comfort food in a comfortable limousine . . . you
name it, you can have the most comfortable one.
And who doesn't want to be more comfortable,

especially when we are in emotional or physical pain? But the truth is that comfort teaches us nothing, whereas there is much to learn from our pain and discomfort. The challenge is not merely enduring pain, but rather finding a way for the pain we suffer and the pain we witness to change our lives forever and for the better.

"How was Africa?" many people asked after I returned from my congregation's volunteer mission to help build a series of vegetable stalls outside a small Ugandan village. Ugandan women who sell their garden vegetables on the roadside alone are vulnerable to attack. Constructing several stalls all together makes everyone safer. "Was it fun?" people wanted to know. "Did you see the gorillas and the elephants?"

I am a man of words, and yet I had no words with which to answer those questions. How could I describe a country where 85 percent of all children are either physically or sexually abused and where, on the walls of the schools I visited, there were slogans painted everywhere like *Scream when you are attacked* and *Silence will kill you*? How can I describe walking through an AIDS clinic that had no supplies of any kind—not an aspirin, not a bed, not a bandage, nothing—because graft and corruption siphon everything off at the top? Everywhere I looked in the orphanages, I saw young children with even younger children on their backs, raising their own siblings because their parents had died of AIDS. Little distended bellies, infected eyes, and no one who cared. I met a grandmother who supported her entire family with a few chickens and their eggs. A widow with three young children, barely more than a child herself, with one gaunt cow that produced a dollar's worth of milk a day—that's it. That's what she had to keep her family alive.

"I am uncomfortable because I can do so little. I am uncomfortable because I can do so much."

Here's the final entry in my journal from that mission. These are the only words I could manage:

What can I do other than to notice you; so black, so chocolate surrounding the white of your eyes and your teeth? So beautiful and alive, you precious children following me like a gaggle of geese, reaching for my hand—so beautiful, so terrible, so thin, so infected, so young to carry the water and the sorrow of a continent. What can I do but to notice you?

What can I do but to notice the empty clinic, smelling of urine? What can I bring but my silent apology for my blessed and privileged life? What can I do other than to wonder if I would ever have the strength of a woman surrounded by her chickens, widowed, old, proud, dirty, shoveling shit beneath a dollar-a-day cow, while I nibble my box lunch on the way back to the cool, quiet hotel room where my neatly folded laundry awaits?

I am uncomfortable because I am here. I am uncomfortable because I will not be here. I am uncomfortable because I can do so little. I am uncomfortable because I can do so much. I am uncomfortable because there is so much to say. I am uncomfortable because there is nothing to say. I shall leave you poor children today, but you shall never leave me. You shall, this place shall, make me forever uncomfortable, forever blessed.

Comfort dulls our edge—pain sharpens our perspective. Witnessing or experiencing real pain forces us to cease feigning blindness; to really look at the world and at ourselves. This is pain's greatest challenge and its greatest gift.

People talk a lot about wanting to change the world. I think in a way it's an unrealistic idea because it is impossible for any of us to change the entire world. But we can let the pain we suffer and the pain we witness inspire us to change what we can. Our community. Our family. Or maybe just one life.

YOU MATTER

In the last analysis, the essential thing is the life of the individual. This alone makes history.

— C. G. JUNG

According to a folktale recorded in the literature of all three Abrahamic faiths, Abraham's father, Terah, was an idol manufacturer who once went away and left Abraham in charge of his store. While Terah was away, a man walked in and asked to buy an idol. Abraham asked him how old he was, and when the man responded, "Fifty years old," Abraham said, "You are fifty years old and would worship a day-old statue!" Realizing even a young boy recognized the foolishness of idolatry, the man left, ashamed.

Later, a woman walked into the store and wanted to make an offering to one of the idols.

But Abraham took a stick, smashed all the idols but the largest one and then placed the stick in the hand of the remaining idol. When Terah returned, he asked Abraham what happened to all the idols. Abraham told him that a woman came in to make an offering to the idols. The idols argued about which one should eat the offering first. Then the largest idol took the stick and smashed the other idols to bits.

Angrily, Terah scolded Abraham saying, "They are only statues. They can't move. They have no knowledge and they have no power." Whereupon Abraham asked, "If all of that is true, why do you worship them?"

At this point Terah took Abraham to Nimrod, the local ruler.

Nimrod proclaimed to Abraham that if he thought idols had no power, he should worship fire. Abraham responded that water puts out fire. So Nimrod suggested he worship water. Abraham responded that clouds hold water. Next Nimrod declared he worship clouds. Abraham responded that wind pushes clouds. Then Nimrod declared they worship wind. Abraham responded that people withstand wind.

Finally, Nimrod became angry with Abraham and declared that Abraham should be cast into the fire, saying that if Abraham was correct that there is a real God, that God would save him. Abraham was cast into the fire—and saved by God.

Despite its primitive understanding of idolatry and its fantastical ending, this legend nevertheless makes a very important point about the disruption in thinking that Abraham represents. Before Abraham rejected his father's paganism, most people in most places believed that humans had little power and virtually no freedom to determine their own path. Pagans believed in an existence that was inevitably cyclical, thinking that all humans were part of a cycle that would repeat itself over and over and over again throughout all time. The idea that individuals mattered, that they could change things, that existence was a linear journey toward what could be made an ever better world—that was a big, radical, idol-smashing, powerful idea. It still is, and it's needed now more than ever before in human history.

Consider this chilling illustration of just how far away we are moving from the powerful idea that people matter. "One day . . . a woman who had lost a child was talking to a robot in the shape of a baby seal," says researcher Sherry Turkle about her work in nursing homes. "It seemed to be looking in her eyes. It seemed to be following the conversation. It comforted her. And many people found this amazing. But that woman was trying to make sense of her life with a machine that had no experience of the arc of a human life. That robot put on a great show.

"I didn't find it amazing," the researcher admitted. "I found it one of the most wrenching, complicated moments in my 15 years of work. But when I stepped back, I felt myself at the cold, hard center of a perfect storm. We expect more from technology and less from each other. And I ask myself, 'Why have things come to this?'"

Another commentator, Shelley Podolny, put it this way: "Our phones can speak to us (just as a human would). Our home appliances can take commands (just as a human would). Our cars will be able to drive themselves (just as a human would)." When most of the time we are communicating with algorithms and they with us, Podolny asks, "What does 'human' even mean?" How much do humans even matter? Add to this dehumanization the enormous depression, suffering, and hopelessness that accompany pain, and we can often feel that the answer to the existential human question of how much we matter is "not much."

What I say to those of us who are suffering is just the opposite. What a suffering person deserves to know and to feel—what we all deserve to know and to feel—can be summed up in the two-word truth Abraham brought to the world: *You matter.*

Your pain is proof that you can matter more. Pain is permission to take care of yourself. Pain is a plea to rebalance your life. Pain is an invitation to change, a great liberator proclaiming that unlike the pagans who preceded Abraham, we need not be slaves to yesterday's ways. Pain can wake us up, reminding us that we are free and that what we do with our freedom matters.

What do we do with our freedom born of pain? Ask most people what are the first and second most important things in their lives, and you will almost always get the same answer: family and work. Ask what is third and you begin to get a true measure of that person. Are you proud of what's third in your life? Is it uplifting and meaningful? Or is it eating, dieting, drinking, vaping, shopping, spinning, or Netflixing to excess? Now that you have suffered pain, will there be something different and better in third place? Will it be compassion for others who suffer? Will it be compassion for yourself, your body, your spirit? Will it be a new embrace of life and the people you love?

"The most advanced robot on earth cannot begin to approach who you are and what you can bring to others because of what your pain has taught you."

Pain teaches many things; hopefully most of all it inspires us to add meaning and love to a world where we use robots to fake empathy. Let your pain remind you every day that you matter—and that every person in pain (which means every person everywhere) matters. You matter to your family. They love you and they will always love you. You matter because you were created unlike any other person on earth. This means you have a unique way of loving and teaching and leading and touching and caring for other people that no one else has ever had or will ever have.

Let me say that again. You matter because you were created in a way unlike any other person on earth. You are unique. Your pain, your wounds, your scars and weakness have made you kind, powerful, gentle, and wise in new ways; they have made you beautiful in a way unlike anyone else. The most advanced robot on earth cannot begin to approach who you are and what you can bring to others because of what your pain has taught you. Do not come out of hell empty-handed. Do not let your suffering be in vain. You matter. Live like it.

FIX SOMETHING

We had a kettle; we let it leak.
Our not repairing made it worse.
We haven't had any tea for a week . . .
The bottom is out of the Universe.

— RUDYARD KIPLING

My mom tried her best to say it casually, but it was still such a painful sentence: "Steven, honey, now that Dad is in the nursing home and the town house is sold, before I give everything away, you should go downstairs in the basement and take whatever you want."

My dad was not a materialistic guy. He worried about money his entire life and therefore rarely bought anything that was nonessential—to the point that even after he made it in business, he still reused his dental floss—after all, why throw away a perfectly good piece? And don't get me started on the used tea bags wrapped in paper napkins that he pulled out of his shirt pocket while asking the waitress for "just a little hot water."

So what was left in the basement from a guy who wanted so little? There was his tackle box, still filled with the lures, the sinkers and leaders, the hooks and bobbers from when I was a little boy and he rowed the boat across the lake on those rare Sundays he took me and my little brother, Greg, fishing for blue gills. He was tan, and young, and rowed like the strongest man in the world. But did I want his tackle box? What would I do with it? There aren't any blue gills in LA.

There on a shelf, the gray quilted long underwear he wore when he worked outside in the Minnesota cold at Leder Brothers Metal. Memories of dad at the junkyard washed over me. The noise, the dirt, the heat, the cold. Coming home with frostbitten fingers and toes after days in subzero weather making bales of aluminum and copper. I remember him lying in the bathtub before dinner just trying to thaw out—to soak off the grease and get warm again.

My parents, barely high-school educated, married at 17 and 18 in order to flee their terribly abusive parents. With no idea that children like to be tucked in and read to at bedtime, or should have toys, or want to be asked about school, they nevertheless had the five of us before they were 30.

My dad often made me cry. Rules were military strict, punishment was swift, and the worst thing you could be was a *ligner*—Yiddish for liar. But Dad's toughness and that junkyard put five kids through college and supported the eight family members he brought over from Chile when they had to flee the socialists. Four of them moved in with the seven of us in our three-bedroom home. Four moved in two houses down the block with Uncle Mort and his family of four in their three-bedroom house.

Somehow, no matter how dirty, how cold, how hard—Dad made things work. And not just mechanical things. He was a blue-collar guy who lived in the world of *shvartze* jokes and fag jokes, then turned his entire worldview around to walk my gay brother down the aisle at his wedding. He was so strong. But what would I do with his stack of long underwear in LA?

Then I saw it. The chest of drawers in the back—the one with the broken handles. And there they were—used, rusted, oily, older than my earliest childhood memories—my dad's tools. Another rush of memories. Weekends and summers working with Dad while he fixed things at the handful of buildings he bought over the years with cash from the junkyard. One look at that chest and I was riding again in his dirty gray Oldsmobile with that trunk full of old tools and a plunger.

I rode shotgun as we drove around Minneapolis on our way to fix things. Of course, first there were pancakes in the morning at the Town Talk Diner before we attacked the leaky faucet, the stuck door, or the clogged drain. And of course, there was mostaccioli and meatballs at Café D'Napoli afterward for lunch. I was his scrub nurse: "Hand me those pliers. Give me that hammer. Hold the measuring tape right there."

He wasn't good at it and neither was I, but somehow or another, things usually got patched together enough to keep going without having to pay a professional to do the job. I learned some tricks along the way too, like scraping the threads of a screw along a candle before screwing it into a piece of wood. The wax made things go easier with less damage to the wood and my wrist. My dad didn't throw things away, and if he could fix something himself, he did, and if he could do it without anyone getting hurt—so much the better.

I took three tools from the chest of drawers to carry back with me to my life in LA. "That's all?" my mom asked when I ascended the basement stairs after wiping my tears. "Yeah. That's all."

Those tools called out to me from decades long past. His measuring tape and his chalk line—physical metaphors, teaching me as a kid and reminding me as an adult about being a straightforward guy who measured things as they were—"no *mishegas* (nonsense), no *schticklach* (trickery)"—as my dad would put it in Yiddish. And then a pipe wrench with the name Aaron engraved on it. A reminder of how my son, Aaron, and my dad played hardware store together on the kitchen floor.

First Dad laid a towel on the linoleum floor, then he and Aaron set up shop, removing each tool from the chest and displaying it on the towel. My dad was the potential customer—Aaron the salesman.

"What's this called and what's it for?" he'd ask his little freckled five-year-old grandson.

"That's a hammer. It hits nails into wood, Papa."

"How much is it to buy this hammer?"

"Five dollars, Papa."

"Oh, that's too much money."

Eventually the price was negotiated down, the deal for the hammer was done, and it was on to the screwdriver.

One day, Dad pretended to buy this wrench from Aaron and then told Aaron he was giving it back to him as a gift for all time. The deal was sealed when my dad took out his engraver and helped his amazed grandson etch his name—A-A-R-O-N.

> "Most people don't fix much of anything anymore."

My dad's memory and body are nearly gone—he sits and stares silently in his nursing-home wheelchair, asleep in a diaper and a bib; he does not know my name. The work of his hands is done, and now these—his tools—are mine, and Aaron's too.

Most people don't fix much of anything anymore. The toaster, the blender, the folding chair—they break, we shrug, we throw them away and buy a new one on Amazon, to be delivered right to our door. We see the despair on the news, in the papers, and on the off-ramp. We stop, we look, we shrug, we move on. Someone hurts our feelings. We stop calling, we stop caring, we shrug, we move on.

At its best and most useful, pain forces us to look inside ourselves, to see our flaws, our weaknesses, our secret sins of excess and immorality—and then what? Do we merely shrug and move on? We the children, the grandchildren, and the great-grandchildren of people who would not throw away a perfectly good piece of used dental floss often throw away so much and fix so little.

Can we do more with the tools bequeathed to us by our parents, our grandparents, our prophets, psalmists, and sages? Can we do more with the tools of apology and forgiveness, humility and kindness? The lessons pain comes to teach us are the tools that can repair and save our very lives and souls.

Pain is an invitation to fix what is broken in us and in the world—no *mishegas*, no *schticklach*. A straight and true and measured and deeply held promise to strive to be better, not just better off. Pain is a challenge to reach down into the muck of our hurtful, broken family, our broken city, our broken country, and our broken selves, where we hide so much, and to promise that we will blister our hands in the heat and the cold and fix something—not throw him, or her, or it, or ourselves away, shrug and move on.

Many people make promises when they are in pain. They promise never to drink and drive again, never to cheat again in the bedroom or the boardroom, never to take the love of family or friends for granted, to take better care of their bodies, to be more kind, more present, more generous. But when the pain stops, often so too do the promises. If you make promises you do not intend to keep, if you stand before your pain and merely pretend you are committed to fixing what is broken . . . then you are a *ligner* and your pain will lead you only to more pain.

If, on the other hand, you take pain's lessons to heart and use the tools bequeathed to you, the blessings of your freedom, your wealth, your time, your heart and soul, to fix something that is broken, then you will not have walked through hell and come out empty-handed. You will have traversed the Valley of Shadows to be bathed in the light of wisdom and live a more beautiful life. Use your pain to fix something. And don't wait.

Consider James Q. Wilson and George L. Kelling's "broken windows" theory of crime prevention. The theory was based on their observations about the broken windows of an abandoned hospital building in Northampton, Massachusetts.

The building had just a few broken windows at first. But because those first few broken windows went unrepaired, vandals decided to break a few more windows. Eventually, the vandals broke into the building, and because it was unoccupied the vandals became squatters, and the squatters lit fires inside, and the building was ruined beyond repair. If, on the other hand, you are quick to repair something at the first signs of damage, you prevent a lot of pain and loss. You avoid the point of no return.

Oh I know—I know not everything that is broken can be fixed. I know that some families are so dysfunctional for so long that nothing can save them. Some friendships can never be rescued, some betrayals cannot be overcome, some social problems are so deeply embedded they can never be uprooted. Some injuries to our bodies or our souls can't be fully mended.

But I have also seen so many repair so much. The despondent daughter whose mother deprived her of love becomes a loving mother herself whose children feel none of the pain she felt in her own childhood. The son of the tyrannical father tucks his children in at night and lives as a man of peace in his home and his heart. The troubled child who makes it because that one special teacher would not allow her to fail. The addict who has walked those twelve steps, taking a fearless inventory, bravely fixing what was once so terribly broken; who keeps his word and counts the days of sobriety with faith in his capacity to change, to heal, to live, and to love with integrity; and who knows, respects, and bows in deference and obligation to a Higher Power whose strength is so much greater than our own.

The writer Anne Lamott put it this way: "I always imagined when I was a kid that adults had some kind of inner toolbox, full of shiny tools: the saw of discernment, the hammer of wisdom, the sandpaper of patience. But then when I grew up, I found that life handed you these rusty, bent, old tools—friendships, prayer, conscience, honesty—and said, Do the best you can with these, they will have to do. And mostly, against all odds, they're enough."

My tools are dirty, worn, imperfect—etched with the memory of hardship, workaholism, and fear, bequeathed by an imperfect dad I miss so much who worked so hard to fix what could be fixed. A man who measured straight and true, then acted—no *mishegas*, no *schticklach*—never throwing a child, a family, or a used tea bag carelessly away.

Pain calls us to measure ourselves and then to act. We know what we ought to do—pick up the phone, walk those twelve steps, reach out in apology and love. May our suffering be a promise we keep to fix what is broken with the imperfect tools we have been given. They are hard won and precious, these tools given to us by pain, and they are enough to fix what is broken in our souls and in the world.

THE MELODY OF WHAT REMAINS

*We are healed of a suffering only
by experiencing it to the full.*

— MARCEL PROUST

The violinist Yitzhak Perlman was about to begin a concerto at Carnegie Hall. Just as his bow touched the strings, one of them snapped. Perlman played the entire piece, completely changing the fingerings without missing a single beat. At the conclusion of the concerto, the audience stood and applauded for a long time.

In response, Perlman, who was stricken with polio as a child and now walks with leg braces and crutches, quieted the crowd and simply said, "It is my job to make music with what remains."

"What was beautiful when whole
is beautiful when broken too."

I know that you are suffering. Not only because you have chosen to read this book, but because you are human. We all hurt. We all wound and are wounded. We all walk through some kind of hell. Do not come out of hell empty-handed. Do not let your suffering be in vain. Survive, heal, and grow when your heart or body aches. What was beautiful when whole is beautiful when broken too. The soaring bird amazes, but the wounded sparrow evokes an intimate, deeper, more resonant tone within our souls. Make music with what remains of your suffering. Dance and sing to a melody gentler, wiser, and more beautiful than before.

BIBLIOGRAPHY

Abani, Chris. "On Humanity." TED Talk. February 2008. Available at www.ted.com/talks/chris_abani_muses_on_humanity.

Armstrong, Karen. "Let's Revive the Golden Rule." TED Talk. July 2009. www.ted.com/talks/karen_armstrong_let_s_revive_the_golden_rule.

Buettner, Ray. "How Do You Say, I Feel Your Pain." *Ray's Musings*. April 25, 2014. Available at www.raybuettner.com/page/14.

Collins, Francis. *The Language of God: A Scientist Presents Evidence for Belief.* New York: Simon and Schuster, 2008.

Elias, Ric. "Three Things I Learned While My Plane Crashed." TED Talk. March 2011. Available at www.ted.com/talks/ric_elias.

Frankl, Viktor E. *Man's Search for Meaning.* Boston: Beacon Press, 2008.

Hazleton, Lesley. "The Doubt Essential to Faith." TED Talk. June 2013. Available at www.ted.com/talks/lesley_hazleton_the_doubt_essential_to_faith.

Jacobs, A. J. "My Year of Living Biblically." TED Talk. December 2007. Available at www.ted.com/talks/a_j_jacobs_year_of_living_biblically.

Kramer, Stacey. "The Best Gift I Ever Survived." TED Talk. February 2010. Available at www.ted.com/talks/stacey_kramer_the_best_gift_i_ever_survived.

Lamott, Anne. *Traveling Mercies: Some Thoughts on Faith*. New York: Pantheon, 1999.

Marks, Marlene Adler. "The Strongest Link." *Jewish Journal*. July 19, 2001. Available at http://jewishjournal.com/tag/marlene-adler-marks.

McCullough, David, Jr. Commencement speech at Wellesley High School, Wellesley, MA, June 1, 2012. Available at https://theswellesleyreport.com/2012/06/wellesley-high-grads-told-youre-not-special.

Podolny, Shelley. "If an Algorithm Wrote This, How Would You Even Know?" *The New York Times*. March 7, 2015. Available at www.nytimes.com/2015/03/08/opinion/sunday/if-an-algorithm-wrote-this-how-would-you-even-know.html.

Prager, Dennis. Debate with Frank Zindler at the American Atheists Convention, Minneapolis, March 23, 2008.

Reilly, Rick. "Comeback Kid." *Sports Illustrated*. September 5, 2005.

Richeimer, Steven, with Kathy Steligo. *Confronting Chronic Pain: A Pain Doctor's Guide to Relief*. Baltimore: Johns Hopkins University Press, 2014.

Seligman, Martin. *Flourish: A Visionary New Understanding of Happiness and Well-being*. New York: Free Press, 2011.

Semel, Mary, and Anne McCracken, eds. *A Broken Heart Still Beats: After Your Child Dies*. Center City, MN: Hazeldon, 1998.

Schultz, Howard. "Blanket Trust." *Hermes* (Columbia Business School alumni magazine), spring 2001: 18–19. Available at www8.gsb.columbia.edu/articles/sites/articles/files/hermes-spring-2001.pdf.

Telushkin, Joseph. *Rebbe: The Life and Teachings of Menachem M. Schneerson, the Most Influential Rabbi in Modern History.* New York: HarperCollins, 2014.

Trice, Laura. "Remember to Say Thank You." TED Talk. February 2008. Available at www.ted.com/talks/laura_trice_suggests_we_all_say_thank_you.

Turkle, Sherry. "Connected, but Alone?" TED Talk. February 2012. Available at www.ted.com/talks/sherry_turkle_alone_together.

Wolpe, David. *Why Faith Matters.* HarperCollins, 2008.

Zander, Benjamin. "The Transformative Power of Classical Music." TED Talk. February 2008. Available at www.ted.com/talks/benjamin_zander_on_music_and_passion.

ACKNOWLEDGMENTS

Many of the names have been changed, but this book would not have been possible without each of the brave individuals who have allowed me to share their painful stories. You each know who you are, and I thank you.

Thank you to the extraordinary staff and owner of Villa Cora in Florence, Italy, who allowed me such a beautiful place to work quietly and without interruption during the time in which much of this book was created, and to our dear friends Donatella, Fabio, and Barbara for making our stay there possible. Thank you to Andy and Dahlia for allowing me to finish the first draft of this book in the calm of their home in Kauai. Thank you to Brandy Ledford and Cathy Sandrich Gelfond for reading early versions of the manuscript and encouraging me to keep going.

I am grateful to my dear friend Tavis Smiley for bringing me to the attention of the wonderful people at Hay House, and to my agent, Rebecca Friedman, for believing in this book's potential. A thank you to my editors at Hay House: Patty Gift, who truly is a gift, and Anne Barthel, who helped me find the melody in this book. To my copy editor, Rachel Shields, for her excellent refinements.

To be the rabbi of large congregation is a difficult calling, but it is not a thankless one. I am so grateful to the members of Wilshire Boulevard Temple, with whom I have shared a beautiful three decades of life, learning, loss, and love, for the generous ways they have shared their stories and lives with me and for the trustees, who allow me the time necessary to write, think, and grow.

To Betsy, Aaron, and Hannah, who are my life, I give my deepest love.

And finally, although I would not have wished for any of it at the time, my gratitude for all of the pain I have witnessed and suffered, making life more meaningful and precious each day . . .

ABOUT THE
AUTHOR

Rabbi Steven Z. Leder currently serves as the Senior Rabbi of Wilshire Boulevard Temple, a synagogue in Los Angeles with three campuses and 2,400 families.

After receiving his degree in writing and graduating Cum Laude from Northwestern University, and time studying at Trinity College, Oxford University, Rabbi Leder received a Master's Degree in Hebrew Letters in 1986 and Rabbinical Ordination in 1987 from Hebrew Union College, where he went on to teach Homiletics for 13 years. He has published essays in *Reform Judaism*, the *Los Angeles Times*, Beliefnet.com, and *The Jewish Journal*, where his Torah commentaries were read weekly by over 50,000 people; his sermon on capital punishment was included in an award-winning episode of *The West Wing*. He received the Louis

Rappaport Award for Excellence in Commentary by the American Jewish Press Association and the Kovler Award from the Religious Action Center in Washington, D.C., for his work in African American/Jewish dialogue. He is a fellow in the British-American Project and in 2012 presented at the Aspen Ideas Festival.

Rabbi Leder's first book, *The Extraordinary Nature of Ordinary Things*, brought him national acclaim. In *The New York Times*, William Safire called the book "uplifting." Pulitzer Prize–winning playwright Wendy Wasserstein called Rabbi Leder "everything we search for in a modern wise man; learned, kind, funny, and non-judgmental, he . . . finds the true fabric of our spiritual lives." His second book, *More Money Than God: Living a Rich Life Without Losing Your Soul*, received remarkable critical and media attention, including feature articles in *The New York Times*, *Town and Country*, and major newspapers across the country, as well as appearances on ABC's *Politically Incorrect*, NPR, *The CBS Early Show*, *The Dennis Miller Show*, *Tavis Smiley*, *Cavuto and Friends*, *Scarborough Country*, *Fox Family and Friends*, *ABC Overnight*, and more.

Newsweek named him one of the 10 most influential rabbis in America, but to him what is most important is that he's Betsy's husband and Aaron and Hannah's dad. He is also a Jew who likes to fish. Go figure.

Hay House Titles of Related Interest

We hope you enjoyed this Hay House book. If you'd like to receive our online catalog featuring additional information on Hay House books and products, or if you'd like to find out more about the Hay Foundation, please contact:

Hay House, Inc., P.O. Box 5100, Carlsbad, CA 92018-5100
(760) 431-7695 or (800) 654-5126
(760) 431-6948 (fax) or (800) 650-5115 (fax)
www.hayhouse.com® • www.hayfoundation.org

———

Published in Australia by: Hay House Australia Pty. Ltd.,
18/36 Ralph St., Alexandria NSW 2015
Phone: 612-9669-4299 • *Fax:* 612-9669-4144
www.hayhouse.com.au

Published in the United Kingdom by: Hay House UK, Ltd.,
The Sixth Floor, Watson House, 54 Baker Street, London W1U 7BU
Phone: +44 (0)20 3927 7290 • *Fax:* +44 (0)20 3927 7291
www.hayhouse.co.uk

Published in India by: Hay House Publishers India,
Muskaan Complex, Plot No. 3, B-2, Vasant Kunj, New Delhi 110 070
Phone: 91-11-4176-1620 • *Fax:* 91-11-4176-1630
www.hayhouse.co.in

———

Access New Knowledge.
Anytime. Anywhere.

Learn and evolve at your own pace
with the world's leading experts.

www.havhouseU.com

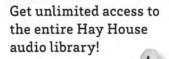